Embracing Sacred Rituals
A path to heart - led transformation

Embracing Sacred Rituals

Copyright © 2023 by E Campbell

All rights reserved. No part of this publication may be reproduced, distributed, or transmitted in any form or by any means, including photocopying, recording, or other electronic or mechanical methods, without the prior written permission of the publisher, except in the case of brief quotations embodied in critical reviews and certain other non-commercial uses permitted by copyright law.

Disclaimer: The information provided in this book is for general informational purposes only. It is not intended to substitute professional advice. The advice and strategies contained herein may not be suitable for your situation. You should consult with a professional when appropriate. Neither the publisher nor the author shall be liable for any loss of profit or any other commercial damages, including but not limited to special, incidental, consequential, personal, or other damages.

Published by The Lotus Heart Publishing Co.
ISBN: 978-0-6459504-0-3
First Edition: 2023

The moral rights of the author have been asserted.

www.embracingsacredrituals.com

This book is dedicated
to the reader's heart.

May it always reside in love with you.

CONTENTS

01

CULTIVATING LOVING AWARENESS
AND MANIFESTING DESIRES
THROUGH SACRED RITUALS

02

NURTURING THE SOUL
THROUGH CHANGE,
GRIEF AND LOSS

03

EMBRACING SACRED CONNECTION
AND COLLECTIVE TRANSFORMATION

04

FIVE MINUTE MORNING
SACRED RITUALS

TABLE OF CONTENTS

Introduction..03

Chapter 1

Cultivating Loving Awareness and Manifesting Desires through Sacred Rituals

1.1 Crystal Ritual for Releasing Karma and Embracing a Heart-Led Existence..08

1.2 Crystal Manifestation Ritual: Harnessing the Power of Desires..12

1.3 Shield of Light: Sacred Ritual for Protection 16

1.4 Sacred Ritual for Clarity: A Meditation and Ritual to Aid with Clarity..20

1.5 Nature-Guided Ritual: Connecting with Your Heart's True Purpose..24

1.6 Crystal Infused Ritual: Expanding Loving Awareness.........27

1.7 Dream Weaver Ritual: Lucid Dreaming 30

1.8 Crystal Heart Connection Ritual: Connect With Your Heart Intelligence..35

1.9 Sacred Space Purification Ritual: Cleanse Your Home of Negative Energy..39

1.10 Sacred Ritual of Energy Cleansing: Protection for Divination..43

TABLE OF CONTENTS

1.11 Sacred Heart Ritual: Expanding the Heart's Energetic Ability..47

1.12 Sacred Bedtime Ritual: Nurturing Astral Travel during Sleep...50

1.13 Sacred Fire Ritual: Honouring Endings and Embracing Transformation...54

1.14 Shamanic Drum Journey: Awakening Inspiration and Altered Consciousness..58

1.15 Shamanic Ritual: Meeting Your Animal Spirit Guide and Embracing Its Wisdom...62

Chapter 2:

Nurturing the Soul through Change, Grief, and Loss

2.1 Inviting Pure Loving Energy: A Heart-Based Meditation for Healing and Clearing...68

2.2 Energetic Cleansing: A Sacred Ritual for Clearing Past Trauma..72

2.3 The Harmonic Expansion: A Sacred Ritual of Peace and Love..76

2.4 Crystal Healing Ritual: Nurturing Recovery and Healing from Trauma...80

TABLE OF CONTENTS

2.5 Embracing Change: A Heart-Centred Ritual with Nature, Shamanic Drumming, and Crystal Grids..................................84

2.6 Sacred Ritual of Remembrance: Honouring a Beloved Departed Soul..88

2.7 Solace Within: A Sacred Ritual to Ease Loneliness and Cultivate Self-Connection..92

2.8 Sacred Ritual of Soulmate Connection: Inviting Love and Alignments 99

2.9 Sacred Ritual for Heart Healing and Spiritual Growth: The Transformational Alchemy of Love...103

Chapter 3:
Embracing Sacred Connection and Collective Transformation

3.1 Sacred Cacao Ceremony: Nurturing Connection and Empowerment In Women's Circles..110

3.2 Sacred Pregnancy Circle Ritual: Nurturing the Divine Feminine..114

3.3 Blessing Ceremony for a Newborn and Mother: Embracing Love, Protection, and Abundance..120

3.4 Awakening Unity: A Sacred Ritual for Spiritual Retreats.128

3.5 Harmonic Healing: A Sacred Soundbath.........................132

TABLE OF CONTENTS

3.6 Embracing Unity: A Sacred Commitment Ceremony with Hand Binding and Nature..136

3.7 Sacred Ritual for Men's Circle: Honouring Masculinity and Facilitating Healing..145

Chapter 4:
Five-Minute Morning Sacred Rituals

4.1 Embracing the Sacred Sunrise: A Five-Minute Morning Ritual to Harmonise the Day...157

4.2 Five-Minute Morning Ritual with A Crystal Singing Bowl..159

4.3 Heart-Centred Abundance: A Five-Minute Morning Ritual to Invite Flow and Prosperity..161

4.4 Shielding and Protecting: A Five-Minute Morning Ritual to Protect Your Energy...163

4.5 A Five-Minute Morning Sacred Ritual for Heart Protection...166

4.6 Five-Minute Morning Heart-Based Sacred Ritual for Anxiety Relief..169

4.7 Water Blessing for Pure health and Harmonic Energy:..172

INTRODUCTION

Embracing Sacred Rituals - A Path to Heart-led Transformation

In a world that often feels chaotic and disconnected, where the demands of modern life can leave us feeling overwhelmed and detached from our true selves, there exists a profound need for reconnection. We yearn for a deeper sense of purpose, a more meaningful existence, and a way to navigate the complexities of our daily lives with grace and love.

This book is an invitation, a gentle call to embrace the sacred rituals that have been practiced by countless cultures and spiritual traditions throughout history. It is a guide that seeks to illuminate the transformative potential of practicing rituals and inspire you to invite them into your own life.

As you journey through the book, you will discover that sacred rituals are not confined to any particular religion or belief system. A place, time, object, or ritual set aside for a particular purpose is considered sacred. In many cultures, trees, plants, mountains, deserts, valleys, and rivers are regarded as sacred. These rituals are universal in essence, transcending cultural boundaries and speaking to the deepest parts of our souls. They offer us a language of the heart, a way to express our deepest longings, a pathway to manifestation, and a means to connect with something greater than ourselves.

INTRODUCTION

Embracing Sacred Rituals - A Path to Heart-led Transformation

Through the practice of sacred rituals, we can cultivate a profound sense of presence, a deep connection to our own inner wisdom, and a greater capacity to love and be loved. We can learn to navigate life's challenges with grace and resilience, create the life that is aligned with our heart, and we can find solace and healing in times of sorrow and loss.

So, my love, I invite you to embark on this journey with an open heart and a willingness to explore the transformative power of sacred rituals. May this book serve as a guiding light, illuminating the path towards a more heart-led, loving, and transformative existence. May it inspire you to embrace these practices and encourage you to develop your own rituals further as you discover the profound changes they can bring to your modern life.

May you find solace, joy, and a deeper connection to the sacred as you embark on this transformative journey. May you be blessed with the courage to invite sacred rituals into your life and experience the profound transformation that awaits.

With love and gratitude,

E Campbell x

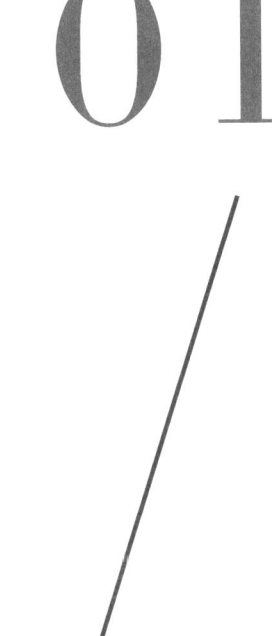

CHAPTER

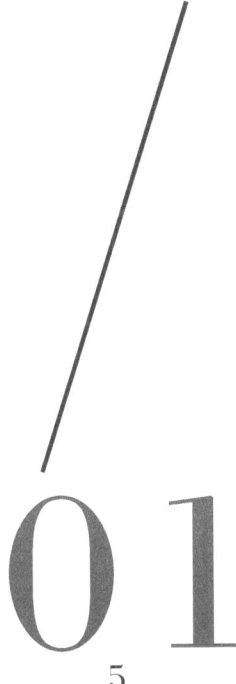

01
CHAPTER

Cultivating Loving Awareness and Manifesting Desires through Sacred Rituals

Deep within our hearts, there exists a profound longing for connection, purpose, and the fulfilment of our deepest desires. We yearn to live a life guided by love, to expand our awareness, and to manifest our dreams into tangible reality. It is within this sacred space of intention and possibilities that we embark on a transformative journey through the rituals within this chapter.

This chapter is a collection of sacred rituals carefully crafted to expand loving awareness, encourage heart-led living, and empower us to manifest our desires into creation. Each ritual is a testament to the inherent power we possess to shape our lives and co-create with the universe.

In the midst of a fast-paced world, rituals can become anchors of presence, reminding us to slow down, listen to the whispers of our hearts, and cultivate a deep sense of gratitude for the present moment. They offer us the opportunity to tap into the wellspring of love within us, to trust in the unfolding of our path, and to surrender to the divine timing of our desires.

As you embark on this journey through the rituals within this chapter, I invite you to approach them with an open heart, an energy of curiosity, and a willingness to surrender to the wisdom of the heart and connected universe. Allow yourself to fully immerse in each ritual, embracing the transformative power they hold and trusting in the process of manifestation.

01
CHAPTER

Cultivating Loving Awareness and Manifesting Desires through Sacred Rituals

May these sacred rituals serve as gentle guides, expanding your loving awareness, igniting your creative fire, and empowering you to manifest your desires into your reality. May they remind you of the infinite possibilities that reside within you and the boundless support of the universe.

May these rituals be a testament to the power of sacred practices in shaping our lives and a reminder that, when we align our mind, heart and actions, we become co-creators of our own destiny.

With love and gratitude.

Crystal Ritual
*Releasing Karma &
Embracing a Heart-Led Existence*

Introduction

Welcome to this sacred ritual that utilises the power of crystals to release karmic patterns and guide you towards living a more heart-led existence. Crystals have long been revered for their energetic properties and ability to facilitate healing and transformation. In this ritual, we will harness their energy to release past karma and reset our path, allowing our hearts to guide us towards a more authentic and fulfilling life. Find a quiet and comfortable space where you can fully immerse yourself in this transformative experience.

Materials Needed
1. Clear Quartz Crystal
2. Rose Quartz Crystal
3. Amethyst Crystal
4. Selenite Crystal
5. Palo Santo or Sage for cleansing
6. A journal and pen

INSTRUCTIONS

1. Preparation
Begin by cleansing your space and crystals. Light the Palo Santo or Sage, allowing the smoke to purify the energy around you. Pass each crystal through the smoke, visualising any stagnant or negative energy being released. Set the cleansed crystals in front of you, ready for use.

2. Grounding and Centring
Sit comfortably, close your eyes, and take a few deep breaths. Visualise roots growing from the soles of your feet, extending deep into the Earth, grounding you firmly. Feel the supportive energy of the Earth beneath you, providing stability and strength. As you breathe, repeat the following affirmation three times:

"I am grounded in the present moment, ready to release past karma and embrace a heart-led existence."

3. Crystal Placement
Place the Clear Quartz Crystal in front of you, representing clarity and amplification of intentions. Position the Rose Quartz Crystal on your heart centre, symbolising love, compassion, and healing. Hold the Amethyst Crystal in your non-dominant hand, representing spiritual growth and transformation. Finally, hold the Selenite Crystal in your dominant hand, signifying purification and connection to higher realms.

INSTRUCTIONS

4. Release and Reset Meditation
Close your eyes and enter a meditative state. Visualise a golden light surrounding you, enveloping your entire being. As you breathe in, imagine this golden light entering your body, filling every cell with healing energy. As you exhale, release any past karmic patterns, negative beliefs, or attachments that no longer serve you. Visualise them dissolving into the golden light, leaving you feeling lighter and freer.

5. Affirmation and Intention Setting
Open your eyes and take the journal and pen. Write down any karmic patterns or limiting beliefs that you wish to release. Acknowledge their presence in your life, but affirm that you are ready to let them go. Once you have written them down, hold the paper close to your heart and repeat the following affirmation three times:

"I release all karmic patterns and limiting beliefs that hinder my growth. I am open to embracing a heart-led existence, guided by love and authenticity."

6. Crystal Activation
Hold the Clear Quartz Crystal in your dominant hand and the Amethyst Crystal in your non-dominant hand. Close your eyes and visualise a beam of white light connecting the two crystals, creating a powerful energetic circuit. Feel the energy flowing through you, cleansing and aligning your mind, body, and spirit. Repeat the following affirmation three times:

"I activate the power within me to release karma and reset my path. I am aligned with my heart's guidance."

INSTRUCTIONS

7. Gratitude and Closing
Express gratitude for the opportunity to release karma and embrace a heart-led existence. Thank the crystals for their assistance and support. Take a moment to journal any insights or emotions that arose during the ritual. Close the ritual by blowing out the Palo Santo or Sage, symbolising the completion of the sacred space.

Conclusion
As you carry the energy of this ritual with you, remember that releasing karma and embracing a heart-led existence is an ongoing journey. Trust in the power of the crystals and your own inner wisdom to guide you towards a more authentic and fulfilling life. May your path be illuminated by love, compassion, and the light of your heart.

Crystal Manifestation Ritual
Harnessing the Power of Desires

Introduction

This sacred ritual combines the ancient wisdom of crystals with the power of intention to manifest your deepest desires. Crystals have long been revered for their energetic properties and ability to amplify our intentions. By following this ritual, you will create a sacred space, connect with the energy of specific crystals, and align your intentions with the universe to manifest your desires.

Materials Needed

1. Clear quartz crystal: Amplifies intentions and enhances manifestation.
2. Citrine crystal: Attracts abundance and prosperity.
3. Rose quartz crystal: Promotes love, self-acceptance, and emotional healing.
4. Amethyst crystal: Enhances spiritual connection and intuition.
5. Pen and paper: To write down your desires and intentions.
6. Candle: Represents the element of fire and symbolizes transformation.
7. Matches or lighter: To light the candle.
8. Incense or sage: To cleanse the space and create a sacred atmosphere.
9. Comfortable and quiet space: Where you can perform the ritual without interruptions.

INSTRUCTIONS

1. Preparation
- Find a quiet and comfortable space where you can perform the ritual without distractions.
- Cleanse the space by lighting the incense or sage, allowing the smoke to purify the area.
- Set your intention for the ritual, focusing on what you desire to manifest.

2. Creating Sacred Space
- Light the candle, symbolising the presence of divine energy and transformation.
- Take a few deep breaths, centering yourself and grounding your energy.
- Close your eyes and visualise a protective bubble of light surrounding you, creating a sacred space for the ritual.

3. Connecting with Crystals
- Hold each crystal in your hands, one at a time, and close your eyes.
- Take a few moments to connect with the energy of the crystal, feeling its vibrations and allowing it to align with your intentions.
- As you hold each crystal, state your desires and intentions clearly and confidently. Visualise them as already manifested, feeling the emotions associated with their fulfilment.

INSTRUCTIONS

4. Crystal Placement
   - Place the clear quartz crystal in front of the candle, representing the amplification of your intentions.
   - Surround the clear quartz with the citrine crystals, symbolising abundance and prosperity.
   - Place the rose quartz crystals around the citrine, representing love, self-acceptance, and emotional healing.
   - Finally, position the amethyst crystals around the rose quartz, enhancing spiritual connection and intuition.

5. Affirmations and Gratitude
   - Take the pen and paper and write down your desires and intentions in the present tense, as if they have already manifested.
   - Read your affirmations aloud, infusing them with gratitude and conviction.
   - Express gratitude to the universe for the manifestation of your desires, trusting that they are already on their way.

6. Closing the Ritual
   - Take a moment to bask in the energy of your intentions and the crystals.
   - Blow out the candle, symbolising the completion of the ritual.
   - Express gratitude once again for the guidance and support received during the ritual.
   - Keep the crystals in a safe and sacred space, allowing them to continue amplifying your intentions.

INSTRUCTIONS

Conclusion

By performing this crystal manifestation ritual with intention, focus, and gratitude, you tap into the powerful energy of crystals and align yourself with the universe's abundance. Remember to revisit your intentions regularly, maintaining a positive mindset and taking inspired action towards your desires. Trust in the process and have faith that the universe will support you in manifesting your deepest desires.

Shield of Light
A Sacred Ritual of Protection

Introduction

The Shield of Light ritual is a sacred practice designed to create a protective barrier around yourself and your space. This ritual combines intention, visualisation, and the power of sacred elements to establish a shield of light that repels negativity and promotes safety and well-being. By performing this ritual, you can cultivate a sense of inner strength and create a sacred space that is shielded from harm.

Materials Needed

1. A quiet and comfortable space
2. Soft cushions or blankets
3. A small table or altar
4. Candles or soft lighting
5. A small dish of salt
6. A clear quartz crystal or any protective stone
7. A feather or fan (optional)
8. A small bowl of water
9. A white candle

INSTRUCTIONS

1. Preparation
   - Find a quiet and comfortable space where you can sit undisturbed.
   - Arrange the cushions or blankets in a circle, creating a cosy and safe space.
   - Place the small table or altar in the centre of the circle.
   - Light the candles or soft lighting, creating a gentle and soothing ambiance.
   - Place the dish of salt, clear quartz crystal or protective stone, feather or fan, bowl of water, and white candle on the table.

2. Grounding and Centering
   - Sit comfortably within the circle, closing your eyes and taking a few deep breaths.
   - Inhale slowly through the nose, and exhale through the mouth, allowing your body to relax.
   - Visualise roots growing from your feet, grounding you to the earth's energy.
   - Set your intention to establish a shield of light that protects you and your space from negativity.

3. Salt Purification
   - Take a pinch of salt from the dish and sprinkle it around the perimeter of your sacred space.
   - As you sprinkle the salt, visualise it forming a protective barrier, creating a boundary that repels negativity.
   - Imagine the salt acting as a purifying agent, neutralizing any harmful energy and promoting a sense of safety.

INSTRUCTIONS

4. Crystal Empowerment
- Hold the clear quartz crystal or protective stone in your hands, feeling its energy.
- Close your eyes and visualise the crystal radiating a bright, white light.
- Set your intention for the crystal to amplify your protective shield and enhance your personal power.
- Place the crystal on the table or altar, allowing it to continue emanating its protective energy throughout the ritual.

5. Feather or Fan Cleansing
- If you have a feather or fan, gently wave it around your body and in the space around you.
- As you do this, visualise the feather or fan dispersing any stagnant or negative energy.
- Imagine the movement of the feather or fan creating a gentle breeze that clears away any harmful influences.

6. Water Blessing
- Dip your fingers into the bowl of water and gently touch your forehead, heart, and hands.
- As you do this, visualise the water forming a shield of light around you, shimmering with protective energy.
- Feel the water infusing you with a sense of calm, clarity, and resilience.

INSTRUCTIONS

7. Candle
- Light the white candle on your altar or sacred space.
- As the flame flickers, set your intention for the candle to represent the divine light that surrounds and protects you.
- Visualise the flame growing brighter and stronger, forming a radiant shield of light that envelops you and your space.

8. Affirmation and Gratitude
- Repeat a protective affirmation, such as: "I am surrounded by love and divine light, protected from all harm."
- Express gratitude for the shield of light that you have created and the protection it provides.
- Take a moment to bask in the energy of safety and well-being that surrounds you.

Conclusion
The Shield of Light ritual empowers you to establish a protective shield around yourself and your space. By performing this ritual regularly or whenever you feel the need for added protection, you can cultivate a sense of inner strength and create a sacred space that repels negativity. May the shield of light you have created serve as a constant reminder of your inherent power and the loving divine protection that surrounds you.

Sacred Ritual for Clarity
A Meditation & Ritual to Aid Decision-Making

Introduction

Welcome to the Sacred Ritual for Clarity. This ritual is designed to help you gain clarity and guidance when you find yourself unable to make a decision. By engaging in this sacred practice, we create a space for deep reflection, inner wisdom, and intuitive guidance to emerge. Through meditation and ritual, we invite clarity to illuminate our path.

Materials Needed

1. A Candle
2. A journal or notebook
3. Pen or pencil
4. Any objects that hold personal significance or represent the situation you need clarity on
5. A quiet and sacred space where you can perform this ritual without any interruptions

INSTRUCTIONS

1. Preparation
Find and gather your items. Sit in a comfortable position, close your eyes, and take a few deep breaths to centre yourself.

2. Setting Sacred Space
Light the candle and place it in front of you. Take a moment to visualise the flame as a symbol of divine guidance and illumination. Set the intention to create a sacred space for clarity and insight to emerge.

3. Grounding and Centering
Bring your attention to your breath. Inhale deeply, feeling the breath fill your lungs, and exhale fully, releasing any tension or distractions. Visualise roots growing from the soles of your feet, extending deep into the Earth, grounding and connecting you to its supportive energy.

4. Opening Meditation
Begin the meditation by focusing on your breath. Allow your breath to become slow, deep, and rhythmic. With each inhale, imagine drawing in clarity and insight. With each exhale, release any doubts or confusion. Continue this breathing pattern for a few moments, allowing your mind and body to relax.

INSTRUCTIONS

5. Meditation Script

Close your eyes and imagine yourself standing at the edge of a calm and serene lake. The water is crystal clear, reflecting the gentle rays of the sun. As you gaze at the lake, you notice a small boat waiting for you. Step into the boat, feeling its stability beneath your feet. Know that this boat will guide you to the answers you seek.

As you sit in the boat, feel the gentle rocking motion as it begins to move across the lake. Allow yourself to surrender to the journey, trusting that it will lead you to clarity. As you glide across the water, notice the peacefulness and stillness that surrounds you.

As the boat reaches the centre of the lake, it comes to a gentle stop. Take a moment to observe your surroundings. Notice the clarity and stillness of the water, mirroring the clarity you seek within yourself.

Now, ask the question or state the situation you need clarity on. Allow the question to resonate within you, without seeking an immediate answer. Trust that the answer will come in its own time.

As you sit in the boat, feel a gentle breeze caressing your face. This breeze carries with it whispers of wisdom and guidance. Listen closely to these whispers, allowing them to penetrate your being. Be open to receiving insights, images, or feelings that may arise.

INSTRUCTIONS

Take a few moments to reflect on the guidance you have received. Allow it to settle within you, knowing that the answers you seek are unfolding in their own perfect way and timing.

When you feel ready, express gratitude for the guidance received. Thank the lake, the boat, and the whispers of wisdom for their presence and support. Trust that the clarity you seek is now within you, and it will continue to unfold as you move forward.

6. Journaling and Reflection
Open your eyes and take your journal or paper and pen. Begin writing down any insights, images, or feelings that arose during the meditation. Reflect on the guidance received and how it relates to your situation. Allow yourself to explore any new perspectives or possibilities that have emerged.

7. Closing the Ritual
Take a moment to express gratitude for the clarity and guidance received. Blow out the candle, symbolising the completion of the ritual. Know that the clarity you seek is now within you, and you can access it whenever you need.

Conclusion
The Sacred Ritual for Clarity provides a space for deep reflection, inner wisdom, and intuitive guidance to emerge. By engaging in this ritual, we invite clarity to illuminate our path and aid in decision-making. May the insights and guidance received during this ritual empower you to make choices aligned with your highest good and bring clarity to your journey.

Nature-Guided Ritual
Connecting with Your Heart's True Purpose

Introduction

This sacred ritual is designed to help you connect with your heart's true purpose by using nature as your guide. Nature has a way of reflecting our innermost desires and providing clarity and guidance. By immersing yourself in the natural world, you can tap into its wisdom and align with your authentic path. This ritual can be performed alone or in a group setting, and it is recommended to approach it with an open heart and a willingness to listen to the messages that nature offers.

Materials Needed

1. Comfortable clothing suitable for outdoor exploration
2. A journal or notebook
3. Pen or pencil
4. Optional: any items that help you feel connected to nature, such as crystals, feathers, or plants

INSTRUCTIONS

1. Preparation
- Choose a location in nature that resonates with you. It could be a nearby park, a forest, a beach, or any natural setting that you feel drawn to.
- Dress comfortably and appropriately for the weather conditions.
- Take a few moments to ground yourself by taking deep breaths and setting the intention to connect with your heart's true purpose.

2. Communing with Nature
1. Begin your journey by entering the natural space you have chosen. Take a moment to observe your surroundings, noticing the sights, sounds, and smells of nature.
2. Find a comfortable spot to sit or walk, allowing yourself to become fully present in the moment.
3. Close your eyes and take several deep breaths, allowing the energy of nature to fill your being. Feel the connection between your heart and the heartbeat of the Earth.

3. Setting Intentions
1. Open your eyes and take out your journal or notebook. Write down any questions or intentions you have regarding your heart's true purpose. Be specific and heartfelt in your inquiries.
2. Hold your intentions in your heart and offer them to nature, asking for guidance and clarity.

INSTRUCTIONS

4. Reflecting and Integrating
1. Find a quiet spot to sit or stand, allowing yourself to reflect on the messages and insights you received from nature.
2. Take a few moments to write down any additional thoughts or reflections in your journal.
3. Close your eyes and visualise yourself fully aligned with your heart's true purpose. Feel the joy, fulfilment, and passion that arise from living in alignment with your authentic path.

5. Gratitude and Closing
1. Express gratitude to nature for its guidance and wisdom. Offer thanks for the insights received and the connection established.
2. Take a moment to ground yourself by placing your hands on the earth, feeling its support and stability.
3. Slowly and mindfully, make your way back from the natural space, carrying the wisdom and clarity you gained with you.

Conclusion
By regularly practicing this sacred ritual, you can deepen your connection with nature and tap into its wisdom to discover and align with your heart's true purpose. Remember to approach this ritual with an open heart, a willingness to listen, and a deep respect for the natural world. Nature has much to teach us if we are willing to listen and learn.

Crystal Infused Ritual
Expanding Loving Awareness

Introduction

This sacred ritual aims to harness the power of crystals to enhance and expand loving awareness among others. By becoming a catalyst of energetic transformation, you will create a heart-centred, loving, and energetic space that radiates love and compassion to those around you. This ritual can be performed alone or in a group setting, and it is recommended to have a clear intention and an open heart throughout the process.

Materials Needed

1. Clear quartz crystal
2. Rose quartz crystal
3. Amethyst crystal
4. Selenite crystal
5. A comfortable and quiet space
6. Optional: candles, incense, or any other items that help create a sacred atmosphere

INSTRUCTIONS

1. Preparation
1. Find a quiet and comfortable space where you can perform the ritual without interruptions.
2. Set up the space by lighting candles, burning incense, or arranging any other items that help create a sacred atmosphere.
3. Take a few deep breaths, centre yourself, and set your intention for the ritual. Visualise the expansion of loving awareness and the transformation it will bring to those around you.

2. Crystal Cleansing
1. Begin by cleansing the crystals to remove any stagnant or negative energies they may have absorbed. You can do this by holding them under running water or smudging them with sage or palo santo.
2. Once cleansed, hold each crystal individually in your hands and set the intention for them to amplify and radiate loving energy.

3. Creating the Sacred Space
1. Place the clear quartz crystal in the centre of your chosen space. This crystal will act as the focal point for the energetic transformation.
2. Surround the clear quartz with the rose quartz, amethyst, and selenite crystals, forming a circle around it. These crystals will enhance the loving and compassionate energies.
3. Take a moment to connect with the crystals, feeling their energy and envisioning them radiating love and compassion.

INSTRUCTIONS

4. Meditation and Energetic Transformation
1. Sit comfortably near the crystal circle, close your eyes, and take a few deep breaths to centre yourself.
2. Visualise a bright, loving light emanating from your heart centre, expanding and enveloping the entire space around you.
3. As you breathe in, imagine this loving light growing stronger and brighter within you. As you exhale, visualise it expanding outward, reaching all those who are in need of love and healing.
4. Allow this loving energy to flow through you, connecting with the crystals and amplifying their energy.
5. Stay in this meditative state for as long as you feel guided, continuing to radiate love and compassion to all beings.

5. Closing the Ritual
1. When you feel ready, gently bring your awareness back to the present moment.
2. Express gratitude to the crystals for their assistance in expanding loving awareness.
3. Slowly and mindfully, disassemble the crystal circle, thanking each crystal individually.
4. You may choose to keep the crystals nearby or carry them with you throughout the day as a reminder of the loving energy you have cultivated.

Conclusion
By regularly practicing this sacred ritual, you become a powerful catalyst of energetic transformation, expanding loving awareness among others. Remember, the more you cultivate love and compassion within yourself, the more it will radiate outwards, positively impacting those around you.

Dreamweaver Ritual
Lucid Dreaming

Introduction

This sacred ritual is designed to create a sacred and intentional space before bedtime, allowing you to enhance your ability to lucid dream while sleeping. Lucid dreaming is the practice of becoming aware that you are dreaming while in the dream state, enabling you to consciously navigate and explore your dreams. By engaging in this ritual, you will set the stage for a deep and transformative dream experience, inviting lucidity and intention into your dream world.

Materials Needed

1. A quiet and comfortable space in your bedroom
2. A dream journal or notebook
3. A pen or pencil
4. Optional: Crystals, essential oils, or other objects that promote relaxation and dream enhancement

INSTRUCTIONS

1. Preparation
   - Create a calm and soothing environment in your bedroom by dimming the lights, playing soft music, or using essential oils known for their relaxation properties.
   - Set aside a few moments to disconnect from electronic devices and external distractions, allowing yourself to enter a state of tranquillity and receptivity.

2. Intention Setting
   - Sit comfortably in your chosen space and take a few deep breaths to centre yourself.
   - Reflect on your desire to experience lucid dreaming and set a clear intention to become aware within your dreams.
   - Visualise yourself in a vivid and lucid dream, engaging with your surroundings and consciously directing the dream's narrative.

3. Dream Journaling
   - Take your dream journal or notebook and pen, placing them beside you.
   - Write down any dreams or fragments of dreams you remember from previous nights, even if they seem insignificant.
   - This practice helps to strengthen your dream recall and signals to your subconscious mind that you value and prioritize your dream experiences.

INSTRUCTIONS

4. Affirmations and Visualisation

- Close your eyes and repeat affirmations related to lucid dreaming, such as "I am aware within my dreams" or "I easily recognise when I am dreaming."

- Visualise yourself becoming aware within a dream, feeling the excitement and empowerment of being in control of your dream experiences.

- See yourself engaging with your dream environment, exploring and manifesting your desires with clarity and intention.

5. Relaxation and Body Awareness

- Lie down in a comfortable position, allowing your body to fully relax.

- Begin a progressive muscle relaxation exercise, starting from your toes and working your way up to your head, consciously releasing any tension or tightness.

- As you relax each muscle group, bring your awareness to the sensations in your body, grounding yourself in the present moment.

6. Bedtime Ritual

- Before getting into bed, hold any crystals or objects you have chosen for dream enhancement.

- Set the intention that these objects will support and amplify your lucid dreaming experience.

- Place the objects near your bed or under your pillow, allowing their energies to infuse your dream space.

INSTRUCTIONS

7. Gentle Breathwork
- Close your eyes and focus on your breath, taking slow and deep breaths.
- As you inhale, imagine breathing in relaxation and tranquillity. As you exhale, release any remaining tension or thoughts.
- Allow your breath to become slow and rhythmic, guiding you into a state of deep relaxation and receptivity.

8. Sleep Induction
- As you drift off to sleep, maintain a gentle awareness of your intention to lucid dream.
- If you find yourself in a dream, practice reality checks, such as looking at your hands or trying to push your finger through your palm, to determine if you are dreaming.
- If you become aware that you are dreaming, embrace the lucidity and engage with your dream consciously, exploring and manifesting your desires.

9. Dream Journaling
- Upon waking, take a few moments to recall and record your dream experiences in your dream journal.
- Write down any details, emotions, or insights that arose during your lucid dream.
- This practice helps to reinforce your connection to your dream world and encourages further lucid dreaming experiences.

INSTRUCTIONS

Conclusion

By engaging in this Dreamweaver Ritual before bedtime, you are creating a sacred and intentional space to enhance your ability to lucid dream. Remember that lucid dreaming is a skill that develops over time, so be patient and persistent in your practice. With regular engagement in this ritual and a genuine desire to explore your dream world, you can cultivate a deeper connection to your dreams and unlock the transformative potential of lucid dreaming.

Crystal Heart Connection Ritual
Connect with your heart

Introduction

This sacred ritual is designed to help you connect with your heart intelligence using the power of crystals. By engaging in this ritual, you will create a sacred space to explore and deepen your connection with your heart's wisdom and intuition. Remember to approach this ritual with an open heart and a willingness to listen to the whispers of your inner self.

Materials Needed

1. Clear quartz crystal
2. Rose quartz crystal
3. Amethyst crystal
4. Selenite crystal
5. A comfortable and quiet space
6. A journal or notebook
7. A pen or pencil

INSTRUCTIONS

1. Cleansing and Charging

- Hold each crystal in your hands, one at a time, and visualise any negative or stagnant energy being released from the crystal.
- You can also cleanse the crystals by smudging them with sage or passing them through the smoke of incense.
- Once cleansed, hold each crystal under running water for a few seconds to further purify them.
- After cleansing, place the crystals under the moonlight or sunlight for a few hours to charge them with positive energy.

2. Preparation

- Find a quiet and comfortable space where you can perform this ritual without any distractions.
- Place a soft cloth or mat on the ground to create a sacred space.
- Gather the crystals mentioned above and place them in front of you.
- Take a few deep breaths to centre yourself and set your intention to connect with your heart intelligence.

3. Creating Sacred Space

- Light a candle or incense to create a sacred ambiance.
- Sit comfortably in front of the crystals and close your eyes.
- Take a few deep breaths, allowing your body and mind to relax.
- Visualise a protective bubble of light surrounding you, creating a safe and sacred space for this ritual.

INSTRUCTIONS

4. Crystal Connection

- Take the clear quartz crystal in your hand and hold it close to your heart.
- Close your eyes and focus on your breath, allowing your awareness to settle in your heart centre.
- Visualise a beam of light extending from your heart into the clear quartz crystal, creating a connection between your heart and the crystal's energy.
- Feel the energy of the crystal merging with your own, allowing your heart intelligence to awaken and expand.

5. Heart Reflection

- Take the rose quartz crystal in your hand and place it over your heart.
- Allow yourself to feel the gentle and loving energy of the rose quartz permeating your heart space.
- Reflect on any emotions, desires, or insights that arise from your heart centre.
- Write down any thoughts or feelings that come to you in your journal, allowing your heart intelligence to guide your words.

6. Intuition Activation

- Take the amethyst crystal in your hand and hold it between your eyebrows, at your third eye.
- Close your eyes and imagine the amethyst crystal activating your intuition and opening your third eye.
- Allow any intuitive insights or messages to flow into your awareness.
- Trust your inner guidance and write down any intuitive messages or visions that come to you.

INSTRUCTIONS

7. Integration and Gratitude
 - Hold the selenite crystal in your hand and place it on top of your head, at your crown chakra.
 - Visualise the selenite crystal infusing your entire being with divine light and wisdom.
 - Take a few moments to integrate the experiences and insights gained during this ritual.
 - Express gratitude for the connection you have established with your heart intelligence and the crystals.

Conclusion
As you conclude this ritual, take a few moments to ground yourself by placing your hands on the ground or envisioning roots extending from your feet into the earth. Express gratitude for the guidance received and trust that your heart intelligence will continue to guide you on your journey. Remember to honour and nurture this connection with your heart intelligence in your daily life.

Sacred Space Purification Ritual
Cleanse Your Home of Negative Energy

Introduction

The Sacred Space Purification ritual is designed to cleanse your home of any negative energy, creating a harmonious and uplifting environment. This ritual combines the power of intention, visualisation, and sacred elements to purify and restore positive energy within your living space. By performing this ritual, you can create a sanctuary that promotes peace, balance, and well-being.

Materials Needed

1. A bundle of dried sage or palo santo
2. A heatproof bowl or shell
3. Matches or a lighter
4. A small dish of sea salt
5. A feather or fan (optional)
6. A bell or chime (optional)
7. A small bowl of water
8. A white candle

INSTRUCTIONS

1. Preparation

- Begin by tidying and decluttering your home, creating a clean and organized space.
- Open windows and doors to allow fresh air to circulate throughout the house.
- Set up a small altar or sacred space in a central location, where you can perform the ritual.

2. Grounding and Centering

- Find a quiet space within your home and take a few deep breaths to centre yourself.
- Visualise roots growing from your feet, grounding you to the earth's energy.
- Set your intention to cleanse and purify your home, releasing any negative energy and inviting positive vibrations.

3. Smudging with Sage or Palo Santo

- Light the bundle of dried sage or palo santo using matches or a lighter.
- Allow the flame to catch and then gently blow it out, allowing the smoke to billow.
- Starting at the front entrance of your home, walk clockwise through each room, wafting the smoke into corners, closets, and doorways.
- As you move, visualise the smoke purifying the space, dispelling any negative energy and replacing it with positive, uplifting energy.
- Pay special attention to areas that feel heavy or stagnant.
- Use a feather or fan to guide the smoke, if desired.

INSTRUCTIONS

4. Salt Purification
 - Take a small pinch of sea salt from the dish and sprinkle it in each corner of every room.
 - As you sprinkle the salt, visualize it forming a protective barrier, absorbing and neutralizing any negative energy.
 - Imagine the salt transforming into pure, radiant light, filling the space with positive vibrations.

5. Sound Cleansing
 - If you have a bell or chime, gently ring it in each room, allowing the sound to reverberate.
 - As the sound resonates, visualise it breaking up any stagnant or negative energy, clearing the space.
 - Imagine the sound waves filling the room with harmonious vibrations, restoring balance and tranquillity.

6. Water Blessing
 - Take the small bowl of water and walk through each room, flicking droplets of water into the air.
 - As you do this, visualise the water cleansing and purifying the space, washing away any residual negative energy.
 - Feel the water bringing a sense of renewal and freshness to your home.

INSTRUCTIONS

7. Candle Visualisation
 - Light the white candle on your altar or sacred space.
 - As the flame flickers, set your intention for the candle to radiate positive energy and light throughout your home.
 - Visualise the flame illuminating every corner, dispelling darkness, and infusing the space with warmth, love, and protection.

8. Gratitude and Closing
 - Take a moment to express gratitude for the cleansing and purification of your home.
 - Thank the elements, the spirits, or any higher power you believe in for their assistance.
 - Blow out the candle, symbolising the completion of the ritual and the sealing of positive energy within your home.

Conclusion
The Sacred Space Purification ritual allows you to cleanse your home of negative energy, creating a sanctuary filled with positive vibrations. By performing this ritual regularly or whenever your space feels heavy or stagnant, you can restore balance, harmony, and a sense of peace within your living environment. May your home be a sacred space that nurtures and uplifts you and all who dwell within it.

Sacred Ritual of Energy Cleansing
Protection for Divination

Introduction

This sacred ritual is designed to create a safe and connective space before engaging in tarot card readings, oracle card readings, or any form of spiritual divination. By cleansing and protecting your energy, you can enhance your intuition, establish clear boundaries, and invite positive and accurate guidance during your divination practice.

Materials Needed

1. Sage bundle, palo santo, or any other cleansing tool of your choice.
2. A small dish or shell to hold the cleansing tool.
3. A white candle or any candle that represents purity and clarity.
4. A crystal that resonates with your intention for protection, such as black tourmaline, amethyst, or clear quartz.
5. Optional: Incense, essential oils, or any other items that evoke a sense of sacredness and support the intention of the ritual.

INSTRUCTIONS

1. Preparation
 - Set up a sacred space where you can perform the ritual undisturbed.
 - Place the candle, cleansing tool, and crystal on a small table or altar.
 - Optional: Light incense or diffuse essential oils to create a serene and sacred atmosphere.

2. Grounding and Centering
 - Begin by taking a few deep breaths, grounding yourself in the present moment.
 - Close your eyes and visualise roots extending from the soles of your feet, anchoring you to the earth.
 - Allow yourself to feel connected, stable, and centred.

3. Cleansing
 - Light the candle, symbolising the illumination of your inner wisdom and clarity.
 - Hold the cleansing tool over the flame, allowing it to catch fire briefly, then gently blow it out, creating smoke.
 - Waft the smoke around your body, starting from the top of your head and moving down to your feet.
 - Visualise the smoke purifying and cleansing your energy field, releasing any stagnant or negative energy.

INSTRUCTIONS

4. Setting Intentions
 - Hold the crystal in your hands, close your eyes, and take a moment to connect with its energy.
 - Set your intention for protection, clarity, and accurate guidance during your divination practice.
 - Visualise a shield of light surrounding you, creating a safe and sacred space for your divination work.

5. Affirmations and Prayers
 - While holding the crystal, repeat affirmations or prayers that resonate with your intention for protection and clarity.
 - Examples: "I am surrounded by divine light and protected from any negative influences." or "I open myself to receive accurate and insightful guidance from the spiritual realm."

6. Crystal Placement
 - Place the crystal near your divination tools, such as tarot cards or oracle cards, as a symbol of ongoing protection and connection.
 - Visualise the crystal infusing your divination tools with its energy, enhancing their accuracy and guidance.

INSTRUCTIONS

7. Gratitude and Invocation
 - Express gratitude for the cleansing and protection received during this ritual.
 - Speak an invocation or prayer, inviting your spirit guides, angels, or any higher power you resonate with to support and guide you during your divination practice.

8. Closing and Grounding
 - Once you have completed the ritual, take a few deep breaths to ground yourself.
 - Express gratitude for the sacred space created and the support received.
 - Visualise yourself surrounded by a protective and nurturing energy, feeling empowered and ready to engage in divination with clarity and accuracy.

Conclusion
By engaging in this sacred ritual of energy cleansing and protection, you can create a safe and connective space before using tarot cards, oracle cards, or any form of spiritual divination. Remember to approach this ritual with reverence, intention, and an open heart, allowing the cleansing and protective energies to support and guide your divination practice. Regularly practicing this ritual can help maintain energetic hygiene, fostering a clear and accurate connection with the spiritual realm.

Sacred Heart Ritual
Expanding the Heart's Energetic Ability

Introduction
In the depths of our being, there lies a wellspring of love and compassion, a boundless reservoir of energy waiting to be awakened and shared with the world. This sacred ritual, rooted in ancient wisdom, offers a pathway to expand the heart's energetic ability, allowing us to tap into the infinite power of love and radiate its transformative energy far and wide.

1. Preparation
  - Find a quiet and sacred space where you can be undisturbed. Light a candle or burn some incense to create a sacred atmosphere.
  - Sit comfortably, with your spine straight and your palms resting gently on your lap. Take a few deep breaths, allowing your body and mind to relax.

2. Visualisation
  - Close your eyes and bring your awareness to your heart centre, located in the middle of your chest. Visualise a radiant, golden light glowing within your heart, representing the divine love that resides within you.
  - Take a moment to connect with this divine presence, feeling its warmth and unconditional love enveloping your entire being.

INSTRUCTIONS

3. Expansion

- With each inhale, imagine that you are drawing in this divine love and allowing it to fill your heart centre. Feel your heart expanding with each breath, growing larger and more radiant.
- As you exhale, visualise this expanded heart energy flowing outwards, extending beyond your physical body and reaching out to touch the hearts of all beings around you.
- With each breath, continue to expand your heart's energetic field, encompassing your loved ones, your community, and eventually expanding to embrace all of humanity and the entire planet.

4. Affirmation

- Repeat the following affirmation silently or aloud: "I am a vessel of divine love. My heart's energetic capacity expands with each breath, radiating love and compassion to all beings. I am a channel for transformative love in the world."

5. Gratitude and Integration

- Take a few moments to express gratitude for the love that flows through you and for the opportunity to expand your heart's energetic ability. Offer thanks to the divine presence within and around you.
- Slowly bring your awareness back to your physical body, feeling the energy of your expanded heart centre gently grounding you in the present moment.
- When you are ready, open your eyes and carry the energy of this expanded heart with you throughout your day, allowing it to guide your actions and interactions with others.

INSTRUCTIONS

Remember, this sacred ritual is not a one-time event but a practice to be integrated into your daily life. As you continue to expand your heart's energetic ability, you will find that love becomes your guiding force, transforming not only your own existence but also the world around you.

May this sacred ritual serve as a catalyst for the expansion of your heart's energetic capacity, allowing you to become a beacon of love and compassion in a world that so desperately needs it. May you embrace this practice with reverence and dedication, knowing that your heart has the power to create profound change in yourself and in the world.

With love and blessings.

Sacred Bedtime Ritual
Nurturing Astral Travel During Sleep

Introduction

This sacred bedtime ritual is designed to create a conducive environment for astral travel during sleep. By engaging in this ritual, you can enhance your ability to explore the astral realm, expand your consciousness, and gain spiritual insights while you rest.

Materials Needed

1. Comfortable sleep environment: Ensure your bedroom is clean, clutter-free, and conducive to relaxation and deep sleep.
2. Relaxing essential oils: Choose calming essential oils such as lavender, frankincense, or sandalwood to promote relaxation and enhance your astral travel experience.
3. Crystal companion: Select a crystal that resonates with astral travel, such as amethyst, labradorite, or clear quartz, to keep near your bed.
4. Journal and pen: Keep a journal nearby to record your astral travel experiences upon waking.

INSTRUCTIONS

1. Preparation
 - Create a peaceful and serene sleep environment by tidying up your bedroom and removing any distractions.
 - Dim the lights or use soft, warm lighting to create a soothing atmosphere.
 - Take a few moments to centre yourself and set your intention for astral travel during sleep.

2. Aromatherapy
 - Dilute a few drops of your chosen essential oil(s) in a carrier oil or use a diffuser to disperse the scent in your bedroom.
 - Inhale deeply, allowing the calming aroma to relax your mind and body.
 - Visualise the essential oils enveloping you in a protective and supportive energy for astral travel.

3. Crystal Connection
 - Place your chosen astral travel crystal near your bed or under your pillow.
 - Hold the crystal in your hands and set your intention for astral travel, asking for guidance and protection during your journey.
 - Visualise the crystal's energy merging with your own, creating a harmonious connection.

INSTRUCTIONS

4. Relaxation and Meditation

- Lie down comfortably in your bed, ensuring your body is fully supported.
- Close your eyes and focus on your breath, allowing your body to relax and release any tension.
- Visualise a gentle wave of relaxation flowing through your body, starting from your head and moving down to your toes.
- As you relax, imagine your consciousness expanding beyond your physical body, preparing for astral travel.

5. Setting Intentions

- State your intention clearly and firmly in your mind, affirming your desire to explore the astral realm during sleep.
- Visualise yourself floating out of your physical body, free to explore different dimensions and realms.
- Trust that you will remember and recall your astral experiences upon waking.

6. Astral Protection

- Call upon your spirit guides, angels, or any divine beings you resonate with to protect and guide you during your astral travel.
- Ask for their assistance in navigating the astral realm safely and returning to your physical body upon waking.

INSTRUCTIONS

7. Gratitude and Goodnight Ritual
   - Express gratitude for the opportunity to explore the astral realm and gain spiritual insights.
   - Offer a simple goodnight ritual, such as a prayer or affirmation, expressing your trust in the process and your intention to remember your astral experiences.

8. Sleep and Dream Journaling
   - Allow yourself to drift into sleep, maintaining the intention to astral travel.
   - Upon waking, before fully opening your eyes, take a few moments to recall any dreams or astral experiences you had.
   - Reach for your journal and pen, recording your experiences in as much detail as possible, including any symbols, encounters, or insights.

Conclusion
By engaging in this sacred bedtime ritual, you can create a nurturing environment for astral travel during sleep. Remember to approach this ritual with intention, trust, and an open mind, allowing yourself to explore the astral realm and gain spiritual insights. Regularly practicing this ritual can enhance your ability to astral travel, expand your consciousness, and deepen your spiritual journey.

Sacred Fire Ritual
Honouring Endings & Embracing Transformation

Introduction

This sacred fire ritual is designed to honour and release what no longer serves you, allowing for new beginnings and transformation. By engaging in this ritual, you can symbolically let go of the past, embrace the power of endings, and invite positive change into your life.

Materials Needed

1. Outdoor space or a fire-safe container: Choose a safe location outdoors, such as a fire pit or a designated fire-safe container.
2. Firewood or a bundle of dried herbs: Use firewood or a bundle of dried herbs, such as sage or rosemary, to create the sacred fire.
3. Paper and pen: Write down what you wish to release and let go of during this ritual.
4. Matches or a lighter: Use these to ignite the fire.

INSTRUCTIONS

1. Preparation

- Find a safe and quiet outdoor space where you can perform the ritual undisturbed.
- Set up your fire pit or fire-safe container, ensuring it is away from any flammable objects or structures.
- Gather your firewood or dried herbs and place them within reach.
- Take a few deep breaths, centering yourself and setting your intention to honour endings and embrace transformation.

2. Reflection and Release

- Sit quietly and reflect on what you wish to release and let go of in your life.
- Write down these aspects on a piece of paper, being specific and clear about what you are ready to release.
- Take a moment to connect with the emotions associated with these endings, acknowledging and accepting them.

3. Lighting the Fire

- Ignite the firewood or bundle of dried herbs using matches or a lighter.
- As the flames grow, visualise the fire as a powerful symbol of transformation and renewal.
- Feel the warmth and energy of the fire, knowing that it will assist you in releasing what no longer serves you.

INSTRUCTIONS

4. Offering to the Fire

- Hold the paper with your written intentions and slowly bring it towards the fire.
- As you release the paper into the flames, visualise the fire consuming and transforming the energy of what you are letting go.
- Offer a heartfelt statement or affirmation, expressing your willingness to release and embrace positive change.

5. Witnessing and Letting Go

- Sit or stand near the fire, observing the flames as they dance and transform.
- Allow yourself to fully experience the emotions associated with the endings you are releasing.
- As you watch the fire, imagine the energy of what you are releasing being transmuted into light and love.

6. Reflection and Gratitude

- Take a moment to reflect on the significance of this ritual and the power of endings in your life.
- Express gratitude for the lessons and experiences that have brought you to this point of transformation.
- Offer thanks to the fire for its role in the release and transformation process.

INSTRUCTIONS

7. Closing and Grounding
 - When you feel ready, take a few deep breaths and slowly step away from the fire.
 - Visualise yourself grounded and connected to the earth, feeling the stability and support it provides.
 - Express gratitude for the opportunity to honour endings and embrace transformation.

8. Integration and New Beginnings
 - After the ritual, take time to reflect on the insights gained and the energy released.
 - Consider how you can move forward with a renewed sense of purpose and embrace new beginnings.
 - Trust that the transformation initiated by this ritual will bring positive change and growth into your life.

Conclusion
By engaging in this sacred fire ritual, you can honour endings and embrace transformation in your life. Remember to approach this ritual with reverence, intention, and an open heart, allowing the fire to symbolise the release and transmutation of what no longer serves you. Regularly practicing this ritual can support your personal growth, invite positive change, and create space for new beginnings to unfold.

Shamanic Drum Journey
Awakening Inspiration & Altered Consciousness

Introduction

This sacred ritual utilises the power of a shamanic hand drum to guide you on a journey of altered consciousness, allowing you to connect with the realms of spirit and receive inspiration. By engaging in this ritual, you can tap into your inner wisdom, expand your perception, and open yourself to the flow of creative inspiration.

Materials Needed

1. Shamanic / hand drum: Choose a hand drum that resonates with you.
2. Comfortable and quiet space: Find a peaceful area where you can perform the ritual without interruptions.
3. Optional: Incense, candles, or any other items that help create a sacred and serene atmosphere.
.

INSTRUCTIONS

1. Preparation
- Find a quiet and comfortable space where you can sit or lie down.
- If desired, create a sacred atmosphere by lighting incense, candles, or any other items that help you relax and focus.
- Take a few deep breaths, centering yourself and setting your intention for the ritual.

2. Setting Intentions
- Hold the shamanic hand drum in your hands and close your eyes.
- Set your intention for the journey, focusing on receiving inspiration and guidance from the realms of spirit.
- Visualise yourself opening up to the flow of creative energy and allowing inspiration to flow effortlessly into your consciousness.

3. Drumming Rhythm
- Begin gently drumming the hand drum, creating a steady and rhythmic beat.
- Allow the sound of the drum to guide you into a relaxed and meditative state.
- Focus on the sound and vibration of the drum, allowing it to carry you deeper into your journey.

INSTRUCTIONS

4. Altered Consciousness

- As you continue drumming, let your mind relax and surrender to the rhythm.
- Allow your consciousness to expand, opening yourself to the realms of spirit and the flow of inspiration.
- Release any expectations or attachments to specific outcomes, trusting that the journey will unfold in its own unique way.

5. Journeying

- As you enter an altered state of consciousness, visualize yourself in a natural setting that resonates with you, such as a forest, beach, or mountaintop.
- Explore this inner landscape, allowing your senses to come alive and immersing yourself in the details of the environment.
- Be open to encounters with spirit guides, animal allies, or other beings that may offer guidance and inspiration.

6. Receiving Inspiration

- As you journey, be receptive to any messages, symbols, or insights that come to you.
- Trust your intuition and allow the inspiration to flow into your consciousness.
- Take note of any images, words, or sensations that arise, as they may hold valuable insights and creative ideas.

INSTRUCTIONS

7. Integration and Gratitude
   - When you feel ready, gradually slow down the drumming rhythm, allowing yourself to return to a more grounded state of consciousness.
   - Take a few moments to reflect on the journey and the inspiration you have received.
   - Express gratitude to the spirits, guides, and the drum for their assistance and the wisdom they have shared.

8. Closing the Ritual
   - Gently place the shamanic hand drum aside and take a moment to sit in silence, integrating the journey and the inspiration received.
   - Express gratitude once again for the experience and the guidance received.
   - Slowly bring your awareness back to the present moment, gently opening your eyes.

Conclusion:
By engaging in this sacred shamanic drum journey, you can alter your consciousness and open yourself to receive inspiration from the realms of spirit. Remember to approach this ritual with reverence, trust, and an open heart, allowing the rhythm of the drum to guide you into a state of expanded perception. Regularly practicing this ritual can serve as a powerful tool for accessing your inner wisdom, connecting with the flow of creative energy, and receiving inspiration to support your personal and creative endeavours.

Shamanic Ritual
Meeting Your Animal Spirit Guide & Embracing its Wisdom

Introduction

Welcome to this sacred shamanic ritual, where we will connect with the elements of nature to meet and integrate with our animal spirit guide. Animals have long been revered as powerful teachers and guides in shamanic traditions. Through this ritual, we will tap into their energy, purity, and teachings, allowing their wisdom to guide us on our spiritual journey. Find a quiet and natural space where you can fully immerse yourself in this transformative experience.

Materials Needed

- A small bowl of water
- A candle or fire source
- A feather or incense for air representation
- A small stone or crystal for earth representation
- Optional: Any other objects from nature that resonate with you (e.g., flowers, leaves, shells)

INSTRUCTIONS

4. Invocation and Intention Setting
With sincerity and respect, call upon your animal spirit guide. Speak from your heart, expressing your desire to meet and integrate with its energy, purity, and teachings. State your intention clearly, inviting your guide to reveal itself to you in a way that is meaningful and aligned with your highest good.

5. Journey and Meeting Your Animal Spirit Guide
Close your eyes and enter a meditative state. Visualize yourself walking through a beautiful natural landscape, feeling the presence of your animal spirit guide drawing near. Observe your surroundings, paying attention to any signs or symbols that may appear. Trust your intuition and allow your guide to reveal itself to you. Take your time to connect with your guide, observing its appearance, energy, and any messages it may have for you. Engage in a conversation or simply bask in its presence, absorbing its wisdom and teachings.

6. Integration and Exchange of Energy
When you feel ready, express gratitude to your animal spirit guide for its presence and teachings. Offer a small gift from nature, such as a flower or a leaf, as a token of appreciation. In return, ask your guide to share its energy and purity with you. Visualise a gentle exchange of energy between you and your guide, feeling its essence merging with your own. Allow this integration to take place, knowing that you are now connected to your guide's wisdom and guidance.

INSTRUCTIONS

7. Closing and Gratitude

Slowly bring your awareness back to the present moment. Express gratitude to your animal spirit guide, the elements, and any spiritual guides or higher powers you connect with. Take a moment to journal your experiences, insights, and any messages received during the ritual. Reflect on how you can integrate your guide's teachings into your daily life.

Conclusion

As you continue your spiritual journey, remember that your animal spirit guide is always with you, offering guidance and support. Cultivate a relationship with your guide by regularly connecting with its energy and teachings. Embrace the purity and wisdom it brings, allowing it to guide you towards a deeper understanding of yourself and the world around you. May this shamanic ritual be a transformative experience on your path of spiritual growth.

CHAPTER

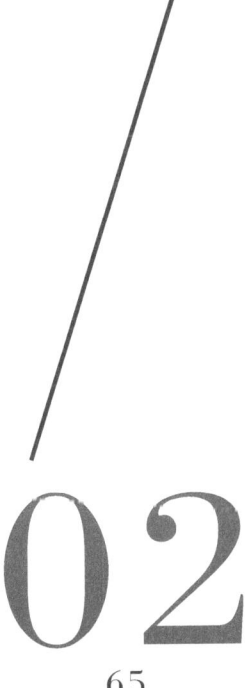

02
CHAPTER

Nurturing the Soul Through Change, Grief and Loss

In the depths of change, grief and loss, when our hearts ache and our spirits feel shattered, we often find ourselves searching for solace and healing. It is during these tender moments that we yearn for rituals that can help us navigate the complex emotions and find a sense of peace amidst the pain.

This chapter is a collection of sacred rituals carefully crafted to provide comfort, support, and a space for healing during times of change, grief and loss. Each ritual is a testament to the resilience of the human spirit and the power of sacred practices to nurture our souls.

Within these pages, you will discover a tapestry of rituals that honour the unique journey of grief, acknowledging that it is a deeply personal and transformative experience. These rituals draw inspiration from various spiritual traditions, ancient wisdom, and the healing power of nature, offering a diverse range of practices to suit different needs and beliefs.

These sacred rituals are not meant to replace the grieving process or diminish the pain we feel. Instead, they serve as gentle companions, guiding us through the labyrinth of grief, reminding us that we are not alone on this path. They provide a framework for self-reflection, remembrance, and the cultivation of inner strength.

02

CHAPTER

Nurturing the Soul Through Change, Grief and Loss

In the midst of grief, rituals can become beacons of light, helping us find our way back to ourselves and reconnect with the essence of our loved ones. They offer us the opportunity to honour their memory, celebrate their life, and find meaning in times of sorrow.

As you embark on this journey through the rituals within this chapter, I invite you to approach them with an open heart and a willingness to embrace the healing power of sacred practices. Allow yourself to be fully present in each moment, surrendering to the emotions that arise and embracing the transformative potential of grief.

May these sacred rituals serve as gentle guides, offering solace, comfort, and a sense of connection to something greater than ourselves. May they remind us that even in the darkest of times, there is a flicker of light, a glimmer of hope, and a path towards healing.

May these rituals be a testament to the resilience of the human spirit and a reminder that, even in the face of loss, love endures.

With heartfelt blessings.

Inviting Pure Loving Energy
*Heart-Based Meditation
for Healing & Clearing*

Introduction

Welcome to the Inviting Pure Loving Energy meditation. In this heart-centered practice, we will embark on a guided visualisation to invite pure loving energy into our lives, heal the heart space, and clear any energetic blockages. By engaging in this meditation, we open ourselves to receive and radiate love, allowing healing and transformation to take place.

Preparation

Find a quiet and comfortable space where you can relax without any distractions. Sit or lie down in a comfortable position, close your eyes, and take a few deep breaths to centre yourself. Allow your body and mind to relax, releasing any tension or stress.

INSTRUCTIONS

The Meditation

1. Grounding and Protection
Visualise roots growing from the soles of your feet, extending deep into the Earth. Feel the grounding energy of the Earth supporting you. Imagine a protective bubble of light surrounding you, shielding you from any external influences.

2. Heart Activation
Place your hands over your heart centre, in the middle of your chest. Take a few moments to focus on your breath, allowing it to deepen and slow down. As you breathe, imagine a warm, radiant light glowing within your heart centre. Feel this light expanding with each breath, filling your entire being with love and compassion.

3. Setting Intentions
Silently or aloud, set your intention to invite pure loving energy into your life. State your desire to heal the heart space and clear any energetic blockages. Trust that this meditation will create a space for healing and transformation.

4. Opening the Heart Space
Visualise your heart centre as a beautiful, radiant flower bud. As you continue to breathe deeply, imagine this flower bud gently opening, revealing a vibrant and luminous heart space. Feel the warmth and expansiveness within your heart.

INSTRUCTIONS

5. Inviting Pure Loving Energy
Imagine a beam of pure loving energy descending from above, entering through the crown of your head, and flowing into your heart space. Feel this energy as a warm, golden light, filling your heart with love, compassion, and healing. Allow this energy to expand and radiate throughout your entire being.

6. Healing and Clearing
As the pure loving energy fills your heart space, visualise it gently dissolving any energetic blockages or barriers that may be present. See these blockages being transformed into pure love and light. Feel a sense of release and freedom as your heart space becomes clear and open.

7. Self-Love and Forgiveness
Direct the loving energy towards yourself. Offer yourself forgiveness, compassion, and acceptance. Embrace any parts of yourself that may need healing or nurturing. Allow the loving energy to envelop you, reminding you of your inherent worthiness and deservingness of love.

8. Sending Love to Others
Expand the loving energy from your heart space to encompass your loved ones, friends, and all beings. Visualise this energy radiating outwards, touching and healing the hearts of others. Send love, compassion, and healing to those who may be in need.

.

INSTRUCTIONS

9. Returning to the Present
Slowly bring your awareness back to your physical body. Feel the ground beneath you, the air on your skin, and the gentle rise and fall of your breath. Wiggle your fingers and toes, allowing yourself to fully return to the present moment.

10. Reflection and Action
When you are ready, take a few moments to reflect on the experience and insights gained during this meditation. Consider how you can integrate the pure loving energy into your daily life, relationships, and interactions with others. Commit to nurturing and honouring your heart space.

Conclusion
The Inviting Pure Loving Energy meditation provides a heart-centred space to invite love, heal the heart space, and clear energetic blockages. By engaging in this meditation, we open ourselves to receive and radiate pure love, allowing healing and transformation to take place. May the love and light within your heart guide you on your journey of self-discovery, healing, and connection with others.

.

Energetic Cleansing
A Sacred Ritual for Clearing Past Trauma

Introduction

This sacred ritual, inspired by Reiki principles, aims to facilitate the clearing of past energetic trauma from the body. It focuses on creating a safe and sacred space for healing, releasing stagnant energy, and inviting in renewed vitality and balance.

The sacred ritual of clearing past trauma is a transformative practice that holds immense power and significance. This ritual aims to release the emotional burdens and wounds of the past, allowing individuals to heal and move forward with renewed strength and clarity. The benefits of this ritual extend beyond the individual, as it can also foster healthier relationships, improved mental and emotional well-being, and a greater connection to one's authentic self. Through the intentional release of past trauma, this sacred ritual opens the door to a brighter and more empowered future.

Materials Needed

1. Comfortable and quiet space
2. Cushions, mats, or a comfortable chair for seating
3. Soft lighting or candles
4. Optional: Crystals (such as clear quartz or amethyst) and essential oils (such as lavender or frankincense)

INSTRUCTIONS

1. Preparation
 - Find a serene and undisturbed space where the ritual can take place.
 - Arrange the cushions, mats, or chairs in a circle or any configuration that promotes relaxation and comfort.
 - Set up soft lighting or candles to create a calming ambiance.
 - If desired, place crystals and essential oils nearby to enhance the energetic environment.

2. Grounding and Centering
 - Begin by finding a comfortable seated position in the designated space.
 - Close your eyes, take a few deep breaths, and allow your body and mind to relax.
 - Visualise roots extending from the base of your spine, grounding you deep into the earth.

3. Invocation and Intention Setting
 - Offer a short invocation or prayer, calling upon divine or spiritual energies that resonate with you.
 - Set your intention for the ritual, focusing on releasing past energetic trauma and inviting in healing and balance.

.

INSTRUCTIONS

4. Self-Reiki
 - Place your hands gently on your body, starting with your heart centre.
 - Allow the energy to flow through your hands, visualising it as a warm, healing light.
 - Move your hands to different areas of your body, intuitively following any areas that feel tense, heavy, or in need of attention.
 - Spend extra time on these areas, allowing the Reiki energy to dissolve any energetic blockages or trauma.

5. Energetic Release
 - Visualise the past energetic trauma as a dark cloud or heavy weight within your body.
 - With each exhale, imagine releasing this energy, allowing it to dissolve and disperse into the universe.
 - As you inhale, envision pure, healing light entering your body, filling the spaces where the trauma once resided.

6. Affirmations and Mantras
 - Repeat affirmations or mantras that resonate with your intention for healing and release.
 - Examples include "I release all past energetic trauma from my body and spirit," "I am worthy of healing and balance," or any other affirmations that resonate with you.

INSTRUCTIONS

7. Visualisation and Cleansing
 - Envision a gentle waterfall of pure, cleansing light flowing over your body, washing away any residual energetic debris.
 - Allow this light to penetrate every cell, organ, and energy centre, purifying and revitalizing your entire being.

8. Gratitude and Closing
 - Slowly bring your awareness back to the present moment, feeling the renewed energy and lightness within your body.
 - Express gratitude for the healing and release experienced during the ritual.
 - Offer a closing prayer or affirmation, expressing your intention to continue nurturing your energetic well-being.
 - Take a few moments to sit in silence, acknowledging the transformation that has taken place.

Note: This ritual is intended to support your personal healing journey. It is important to honour your own boundaries and comfort levels throughout the process. If you are new to Reiki or energy work, consider seeking guidance from a trained Reiki practitioner or energy healer. Remember to practice self-care after the ritual, allowing yourself time for rest, reflection, and integration.

Harmonic Expansion
A Sacred Ritual of Peace and Love

Introduction

This sacred ritual utilises crystal singing bowls and elements from nature to create a harmonious and expanding energy of peace and love. It aims to cultivate a deep sense of connection with oneself, others, and the natural world.

Harmonic Expansion, a sacred ritual of peace and love that harnesses the ethereal power of crystal singing bowls and support from nature. In this transformative experience, we embark on a journey of healing and restoration, guided by the harmonious vibrations emitted by these mystical instruments. As the resonating tones fill the space, they penetrate deep within our beings, dissolving energetic blockages and inviting profound healing on all levels. Through this practice, we connect with the universal energy of love and unity, allowing it to flow through us and radiate outwards, bringing harmony to our souls and the world around us.

Materials Needed

1. Crystal singing bowls (preferably in different sizes and tones)
2. A quiet and serene outdoor space, such as a garden or park
3. Natural elements like flowers, leaves, stones, or shells
4. Optional: Incense or essential oils (such as lavender or rose).

INSTRUCTIONS

1. Preparation
- Find a peaceful outdoor space where you can perform the ritual undisturbed.
- Arrange the crystal singing bowls in a semi-circle, with the largest bowl in the centre and the smaller bowls on either side.
- Place the natural elements, such as flowers, leaves, stones, or shells, in a beautiful arrangement near the singing bowls.
- If desired, light incense or diffuse essential oils to enhance the ambiance.

2. Grounding and Centering
- Begin by finding a comfortable seated position in the outdoor space.
- Close your eyes, take a few deep breaths, and allow your body and mind to relax.
- Feel the connection between your body and the earth beneath you, grounding yourself in the present moment.

3. Setting Intentions
- Reflect on your intention for the ritual, such as expanding peace and love within yourself and the world.
- Visualise this intention as a radiant light within your heart, growing brighter with each breath.

INSTRUCTIONS

4. Connecting with Nature
- Gently open your eyes and observe the natural elements placed near the singing bowls.
- Pick up one element at a time, feeling its texture, appreciating its beauty, and acknowledging the interconnectedness of all living things.
- As you hold each element, silently offer gratitude for the gifts of nature and its ability to inspire peace and love.

5. Sound Bath with Crystal Singing Bowls
- Begin playing the crystal singing bowls, starting with the largest bowl in the centre and moving outward to the smaller bowls.
- Allow the sound to wash over you, enveloping your entire being in its vibrations.
- As you listen to the sounds, imagine them resonating with the intention of peace and love, expanding and radiating outwards.

6. Affirmations and Mantras
- While the crystal singing bowls continue to play, silently or softly recite affirmations or mantras related to peace and love.
- Examples include "I am a vessel of peace and love," "May peace and love expand within me and around me," or any other affirmations that resonate with you.

INSTRUCTIONS

7. Meditation and Expansion

- Close your eyes and enter into a state of deep meditation, focusing on the sound of the crystal singing bowls and the intention of peace and love.

- Visualise this energy expanding from your heart, filling your entire body, and radiating outwards into the world.

- Imagine this energy connecting with others, spreading peace and love to all beings and the natural world.

8. Gratitude and Closing

- Slowly bring your awareness back to the present moment, feeling the vibrations of the crystal singing bowls gradually fade away.

- Take a few moments to express gratitude for the experience, the natural elements, and the power of sound and intention.

- Offer a closing prayer or affirmation, expressing your intention to carry the energy of peace and love with you throughout your day.

Note: This ritual can be performed individually or in a group setting. If practicing with others, you can take turns playing the crystal singing bowls and sharing intentions or affirmations. Remember to respect and honour the natural elements used in the ritual, returning them to their natural environment after the ceremony.

Crystal Healing Ritual
Nurturing Recovery & Healing from Trauma

Introduction
This sacred ritual combines the transformative power of crystals with intention and self-care to support healing and recovery from trauma. Crystals have long been recognised for their energetic properties and ability to promote emotional and spiritual healing. By following this ritual, you will create a safe and sacred space, connect with the energy of specific crystals, and embark on a journey of healing and self-nurturing.

Materials Needed
1. Amethyst crystal: Promotes emotional healing, spiritual connection, and inner peace.
2. Rose quartz crystal: Encourages self-love, compassion, and emotional healing.
3. Black tourmaline crystal: Provides protection, grounding, and release of negative energy.
4. Selenite crystal: Purifies energy, promotes clarity, and aids in releasing trauma.
5. Pen and paper: To write down any emotions, thoughts, or memories that arise during the ritual.
6. Candle: Represents the element of fire and symbolizes transformation.
7. Matches or lighter: To light the candle.
8. Incense or sage: To cleanse the space and create a sacred atmosphere.
9. Comfortable and quiet space: Where you can perform the ritual without interruptions.

INSTRUCTIONS

1. Preparation

- Find a quiet and comfortable space where you can perform the ritual without distractions.
- Cleanse the space by lighting the incense or sage, allowing the smoke to purify the area.
- Set your intention for the ritual, focusing on healing, release, and nurturing self-care.

2. Creating Sacred Space

- Light the candle, symbolising the presence of divine energy and transformation.
- Take a few deep breaths, centering yourself and grounding your energy.
- Close your eyes and visualise a protective bubble of light surrounding you, creating a safe and sacred space for the ritual.

3. Connecting with Crystals

- Hold each crystal in your hands, one at a time, and close your eyes.
- Take a few moments to connect with the energy of the crystal, feeling its vibrations and allowing it to support your healing journey.
- As you hold each crystal, state your intention for healing and release, acknowledging any trauma you wish to heal from.

INSTRUCTIONS

4. Crystal Placement
- Place the amethyst crystal in front of the candle, representing emotional healing, spiritual connection, and inner peace.
- Surround the amethyst with the rose quartz crystals, symbolizing self-love, compassion, and emotional healing.
- Place the black tourmaline crystals around the rose quartz, providing protection, grounding, and release of negative energy.
- Finally, position the selenite crystal near the centre, purifying energy and aiding in releasing trauma.

5. Journaling and Release
- Take the pen and paper and write down any emotions, thoughts, or memories that arise during the ritual.
- Allow yourself to express and release any pain, fear, or sadness onto the paper, acknowledging the impact of the trauma.
- Once you have written everything down, take a deep breath, and visualise the crystals absorbing and transmuting the negative energy.

6. Affirmations and Self-Nurturing
- Read your journal entries aloud, acknowledging the pain and trauma you have experienced.
- Follow each entry with a positive affirmation, such as "I am healing," "I am worthy of love and peace," or "I release what no longer serves me."
- Engage in self-nurturing activities, such as taking a warm bath, practicing gentle yoga or meditation, or engaging in creative expression.

INSTRUCTIONS

7. Closing the Ritual

- Take a moment to bask in the energy of the crystals and the healing process.

- Blow out the candle, symbolising the completion of the ritual.

- Express gratitude for the guidance and support received during the ritual.

- Keep the crystals in a safe and sacred space, allowing them to continue supporting your healing journey.

Conclusion

By engaging in this crystal healing ritual with intention, self-compassion, and gratitude, you embark on a journey of healing and self-nurturing. Remember that healing from trauma is a process, and it is essential to be patient and gentle with yourself. Regularly revisit this ritual, allowing the crystals to support your ongoing healing journey. Seek additional support from professionals or support groups if needed, as they can provide valuable guidance and assistance along the way. Trust in your ability to heal and nurture yourself, knowing that you deserve love, peace, and wholeness.

Embracing Change
A Heart-Centred Ritual with Nature, Shamanic Drumming, & Crystal Grids

Introduction

The Embracing Change ritual is a heart-centered ceremony that symbolises the acceptance of change using the power of nature, shamanic drumming, and crystal grids. This ritual aims to create a sacred space where we can connect with the wisdom of nature, release resistance to change, and open our hearts to new possibilities. Nature changes with cycles, by engaging in this ritual, we invite transformation, growth, and a deep sense of acceptance.

Materials Needed

1. A quiet and natural outdoor space, such as a garden, park, or forest
2. A shamanic drum or any drum-like instrument
3. Crystals of your choice. It can be useful to use ones that resonate with transformation and acceptance (such as amethyst, labradorite, or citrine) but any personal crystals can be used.
4. Optional: A cloth or mat to create a sacred space for the crystal grid
5. Optional: Incense or essential oils (such as sage or cedarwood) for ambiance

INSTRUCTIONS

1. Begin by grounding yourself. Take a few deep breaths, allowing your body and mind to relax. Close your eyes and visualise roots growing from your feet, connecting you to the Earth's energy.

2. Find a comfortable spot in nature and sit or stand in front of where you will build your crystal grid. Take a moment to connect with the energy of the crystals as you place them in configuration that resonates with you, feeling their vibrations and the intention behind their placement (embracing change with love) .

3. Start playing the shamanic drum or drum-like instrument, allowing the rhythm to guide you into a meditative state. Let the sound of the drum connect you with the heartbeat of the Earth and the wisdom of nature.

4. As you drum, bring your attention to the crystal grid. Visualize the energy of change and acceptance flowing through the crystals, radiating out into the space around you.

5. Open your heart and express gratitude for the changes that have occurred in your life. Acknowledge the lessons, growth, and transformation that have come from these experiences.

6. Take a moment to reflect on any resistance or fear you may have towards change. Allow yourself to feel these emotions without judgment, and then consciously release them, surrendering to the flow of life.

INSTRUCTIONS

7. Stand up and find a natural object in your surroundings that represents change to you, such as a fallen leaf, a flower bud, or a small stone. Hold it in your hands and connect with its energy.

8. Speak aloud or silently express your intention to embrace change and accept the natural cycles of life. Affirm your willingness to let go of resistance and open your heart to new possibilities.

9. Place the natural object on the crystal grid, symbolizing the integration of change into your life. Visualize the energy of acceptance and transformation radiating from the crystals and infusing the object.

10. Take a moment to sit in silence, feeling the energy of the crystal grid and the natural object. Listen to your intuition and trust the wisdom that arises.

11. When you feel ready, express gratitude to nature, the crystals, and the universe for their presence and support. Offer a final beat on the drum to honour the energy of the ceremony.

12. Take a few more deep breaths, grounding yourself once again. Open your eyes and slowly return to the present moment.

INSTRUCTIONS

Conclusion

The Embracing Change ritual provides a heart-centered space to symbolise the acceptance of change using nature, shamanic drumming, and crystal grids. By engaging in this ritual, we invite transformation, growth, and a deep sense of acceptance. May the energy of nature, the rhythm of the drum, and the power of the crystals guide us as we embrace change and open our hearts to new possibilities.

Sacred Ritual of Remembrance
Honouring a Beloved Departed Soul

Introduction

This sacred ritual is designed to create a space of love, remembrance, and honouring for a beloved individual who has passed away. By engaging in this ritual, we can connect with the essence of their spirit, express gratitude for their presence in our lives, and find solace in the memories we hold dear.

Materials Needed

1. A photograph or memento of the departed loved one.
2. A small table or altar to serve as a focal point for the ritual.
3. Candles, preferably white or colours that hold significance for the departed loved one.
4. Flowers or other natural elements to create a sacred and beautiful atmosphere.
5. Incense or essential oils to enhance the ambiance and evoke a sense of sacredness.
6. Optional: Personal items or symbols that hold significance for the departed loved one..

INSTRUCTIONS

1. Preparation
- Set up a sacred space where you can perform the ritual undisturbed.
- Arrange the table or altar with the photograph or memento of the departed loved one as the centrepiece.
- Place candles, flowers, and any other items you have chosen to create a sacred and beautiful atmosphere.

2. Grounding and Centering
- Begin by taking a few deep breaths, grounding yourself in the present moment.
- Close your eyes and visualize a warm, loving light surrounding you, providing comfort and support.

3. Invocation
- Light the incense or diffuse essential oils, allowing the fragrance to fill the space.
- Speak an invocation or prayer, inviting the presence of the departed loved one into the sacred space.
- Express your intention to honour and remember them with love, gratitude, and reverence.

INSTRUCTIONS

4. Sharing Memories
- Take a moment to reflect on cherished memories and qualities of the departed loved one.
- Share these memories aloud, speaking from the heart and allowing emotions to flow freely.
- Encourage others present to share their own memories, creating a space of collective remembrance.

5. Lighting the Candle
- Light a candle in honour of the departed loved one, symbolising their eternal light and presence.
- As you light the candle, visualise their spirit being illuminated and surrounded by love and peace.
- Take a moment to silently offer gratitude for the impact they had on your life and the lives of others.

6. Offering
- If there are personal items or symbols that hold significance for the departed loved one, place them on the altar as an offering.
- This could include their favourite flowers, a special piece of jewellery, or any other item that represents their essence.

7. Reflection and Meditation
- Take a few moments of silence to reflect on the presence of the departed loved one and the memories shared.
- Close your eyes and allow their energy and essence to envelop you, feeling their love and guidance.
- Offer any prayers, affirmations, or messages you wish to convey to them.

INSTRUCTIONS

8. Gratitude and Release
 - Express gratitude for the time you shared with the departed loved one and the impact they had on your life.
 - Acknowledge any emotions that arise, allowing yourself to feel and release them with love and acceptance.
 - Visualise the departed loved one surrounded by a loving light, knowing that they are at peace.

9. Closing and Grounding
 - Conclude the ritual by offering a final prayer or affirmation, expressing gratitude for the sacred time spent honouring the departed loved one.
 - Blow out the candle, symbolising the completion of the ritual and the return to the present moment.
 - Take a few deep breaths, grounding yourself in the here and now, knowing that the love and memories shared will always remain.

Conclusion
By engaging in this sacred ritual of remembrance, we can honour and celebrate the life of a departed loved one, finding solace, healing, and connection in the memories we hold dear. Remember to approach this ritual with reverence, love, and an open heart, allowing the space to be filled with the essence of the departed loved one. Regularly practicing this ritual can provide ongoing comfort and support as we continue to cherish their memory and carry their spirit in our hearts.

Solace Within
A Sacred Ritual to Ease Loneliness & Cultivate Self-Connection

Introduction

The Solace Within ritual is a sacred practice designed to help individuals ease feelings of loneliness and foster a deeper connection with themselves. This ritual encourages self-reflection, self-compassion, and the cultivation of inner peace. By creating a safe and sacred space, individuals can find solace within themselves and develop a stronger sense of self-connection.

Materials Needed

1. A quiet and comfortable space
2. Soft cushions or blankets
3. A small table or altar
4. Candles or fairy lights
5. A journal or paper and pen
6. A small bowl of dried lavender or other calming herbs
7. A small bowl of water
8. A photograph or object that represents self-identity

INSTRUCTIONS

1. Preparation
- Find a quiet and comfortable space where you can sit undisturbed.
- Arrange the cushions or blankets in a circle, creating a cozy and safe space.
- Place the small table or altar in the center of the circle.
- Light the candles or fairy lights, creating a gentle and soothing ambiance.
- Place the bowl of dried lavender or calming herbs, bowl of water, journal or paper, pen, and the photograph or object on the table.

2. Grounding and Centering
- Sit comfortably within the circle, closing your eyes and taking a few deep breaths.
- Inhale slowly through the nose, and exhale through the mouth, allowing your body to relax.
- Visualise roots growing from your feet, grounding you to the earth, and connecting you to your inner strength.

3. Self-Reflection
- Open your eyes and pick up the photograph or object that represents your self-identity.
- Take a moment to observe it, reflecting on the qualities, experiences, and values it represents.
- Allow yourself to feel a sense of connection and appreciation for who you are at your core.

INSTRUCTIONS

4. Aromatherapy and Calming

- Take a pinch of dried lavender or calming herbs from the bowl and hold it in your hands.
- Close your eyes and inhale deeply, allowing the soothing scent to calm your mind and body.
- Visualise the fragrance enveloping you, creating a sense of peace and tranquillity within.

5. Water Cleansing

- Dip your fingers into the bowl of water and gently touch your forehead, heart, and hands.
- As you do this, imagine the water cleansing away any feelings of loneliness or disconnection.
- Feel the water purifying your thoughts, emotions, and actions, leaving you refreshed and renewed.

6. Journaling and Self-Compassion

- Take the journal or paper and pen and begin writing down your thoughts and feelings.
- Reflect on any moments of loneliness or disconnection you have experienced.
- Practice self-compassion by acknowledging your emotions and offering kind and understanding words to yourself.

INSTRUCTIONS

7. Affirmations and Self-Acceptance
- Read aloud or silently repeat affirmations that promote self-acceptance and self-connection.
- Examples include: "I am enough just as I am," "I am worthy of love and connection," and "I embrace my solitude and find solace within."

8. Closing and Gratitude
- Take a moment to express gratitude for this sacred time you have dedicated to yourself.
- Thank yourself for showing up and nurturing your self-connection.
- Blow out the candles or fairy lights, symbolising the completion of the ritual.

Conclusion
The Solace Within ritual provides a sacred space for individuals to ease feelings of loneliness and cultivate a deeper connection with themselves. By engaging in this ritual regularly, individuals can develop a stronger sense of self-connection, find solace within their own being, and embrace the beauty of solitude. This practice serves as a reminder that we are never truly alone when we have a deep and loving connection with ourselves.

Solace Within
Sacred Meditation Script

Find a quiet and comfortable space where you can relax and be undisturbed. Sit or lie down in a position that feels comfortable for you. Close your eyes and take a deep breath in, filling your lungs with fresh air, and exhale slowly, releasing any tension or stress.

As you continue to breathe deeply, bring your attention to the sensations in your body. Notice the rise and fall of your chest with each breath. Feel the weight of your body supported by the surface beneath you. Allow yourself to fully arrive in this present moment.

Now, imagine yourself in a peaceful and serene place in nature. It could be a beautiful beach, a tranquil forest, or a serene mountaintop. Visualise the surroundings, noticing the colours, sounds, and scents of this peaceful place. Feel the gentle breeze on your skin and the warmth of the sun on your face.

As you immerse yourself in this tranquil setting, become aware of any feelings of loneliness or isolation that may be present within you. Acknowledge these feelings with compassion and understanding, knowing that it is natural to experience them from time to time.

Solace Within
Sacred Meditation Script

Now, imagine a soft, warm light emanating from your heart centre. This light represents the love and connection that resides within you. With each breath, feel this light expanding, filling your entire body with a sense of warmth and comfort.

As this light continues to expand, imagine it reaching out beyond your physical body, connecting with the energy of the universe. Feel a sense of oneness and interconnectedness with all beings. Know that you are never truly alone, as we are all connected in this vast web of life.

Take a moment to reflect on the relationships and connections you have in your life. Focus on the love and support that exists within these connections. Feel gratitude for the people who have touched your life and brought joy and companionship.

Now, bring your attention back to the light within your heart. Allow it to radiate outward, sending love and compassion to yourself. Embrace your own company and find solace within. Know that you are enough, and your own presence is a gift.

Take a few moments to bask in this feeling of self-love and connection. Allow it to fill every cell of your being, soothing any feelings of loneliness or isolation. Know that you are always supported and loved, both by yourself and by the universe.

Solace Within
Sacred Meditation Script

When you are ready, gently bring your awareness back to your physical body. Wiggle your fingers and toes, and slowly open your eyes. Carry this sense of solace and self-love with you throughout your day, knowing that you are always connected and never truly alone.

.

Sacred Ritual of Soul Mate Connection
Inviting Love & Alignment

Introduction

This sacred ritual is designed to create a space of openness, alignment, and intention to meet your soul mate. By engaging in this ritual, you can cultivate a deep connection with yourself, release any blocks or limiting beliefs around love, and invite the energy of your soul mate into your life.

Materials Needed

1. A quiet and comfortable space where you can perform the ritual undisturbed.
2. Candles, preferably pink or red, to symbolise love and passion.
3. A journal or paper and pen to write down your intentions and desires.
4. Crystals that resonate with love and attracting soul connections, such as rose quartz, rhodochrosite, or emerald.
5. Optional: Incense, essential oils, or any other items that evoke a sense of romance and sacredness.

INSTRUCTIONS

1. Preparation
   - Set up a sacred space where you can perform the ritual undisturbed.
   - Arrange the candles, crystals, and any other items you have chosen in a way that feels visually appealing and energetically supportive.
   - Optional: Light incense or diffuse essential oils to create a romantic and sacred atmosphere.

2. Grounding and Centering
   - Begin by taking a few deep breaths, grounding yourself in the present moment.
   - Close your eyes and visualise roots extending from the soles of your feet, anchoring you to the earth.
   - Allow yourself to feel connected, stable, and centered.

3. Self-Love and Acceptance
   - Take a moment to reflect on your own worthiness of love and connection.
   - Affirm your self-love and acceptance, acknowledging that you are deserving of a soul mate who aligns with your highest good.
   - Repeat affirmations such as, "I am worthy of a deep and fulfilling soul connection" or "I am open to receiving love in its purest form."

INSTRUCTIONS

5. Candle Lighting

- Light the candles, symbolising the illumination of love and passion in your life.
- As you light each candle, state your intentions out loud, infusing them with the energy of your desires.
- Visualise the flame representing the energy of your soul mate, drawing them closer to you.

6. Crystal Connection

- Hold the crystals in your hands, close your eyes, and take a moment to connect with their energy.
- Set your intention for the crystals to amplify your intentions and attract your soul mate.
- Visualise the crystals radiating love and magnetising the energy of your soul mate towards you.

7. Affirmations and Visualisation

- While holding the crystals, repeat affirmations that resonate with your intention to meet your soul mate.
- Visualise yourself in a loving and fulfilling relationship, experiencing the joy, support, and growth that comes with it.
- Feel the emotions of love, gratitude, and excitement as if your soul mate is already present in your life.

INSTRUCTIONS

8. Gratitude and Release

- Express gratitude for the love and connection that is already present in your life, even before meeting your soul mate.

- Release any attachment to specific outcomes or timelines, trusting that the universe will bring your soul mate to you at the perfect time.

9. Closing and Grounding

- Once you have completed the ritual, take a few deep breaths to ground yourself.

- Express gratitude for the sacred space created and the intentions set.

- Visualise yourself surrounded by a loving and supportive energy, feeling open and ready to receive the soul mate connection you desire.

Conclusion

By engaging in this sacred ritual of soul mate connection, you can create a space of openness, alignment, and intention to invite love and meet your soul mate. Remember to approach this ritual with reverence, self-love, and an open heart, allowing the energy of love to flow freely into your life. Regularly practicing this ritual can help align your energy with the vibration of your soul mate, increasing the likelihood of attracting a deep and fulfilling connection.

Sacred Ritual for Heart Healing & Spiritual Growth
The Transformational Alchemy of Love

Introduction

Welcome to the Transformational Alchemy of Love, a sacred ritual designed to support individuals experiencing trauma or difficult times. This ritual aims to heal the heart, infuse the energetic body with love, and facilitate a shift in consciousness for spiritual growth. By engaging in this ritual, we embark on a journey of transformation, transmuting pain into love and expanding our awareness. Find a quiet and comfortable space where you can fully immerse yourself in this healing experience. Let us begin.

Materials Needed

1. A white candle
2. A small bowl of water
3. Rose quartz crystal or any other crystal associated with love and healing
4. A journal and pen
5. Optional: Incense or essential oils for ambiance

INSTRUCTIONS

1. Preparation

Create a sacred space by lighting the white candle and, if desired, burning incense or diffusing essential oils. Take a moment to ground yourself by taking a few deep breaths, allowing your body and mind to relax. Set the intention to heal your heart, infuse your energetic body with love, and expand your consciousness for spiritual growth.

2. Water Blessing

Dip your fingers into the bowl of water and gently touch your forehead, heart, and palms, saying:
"May this water bless and cleanse me, healing my heart and infusing my being with love."

3. Heart Meditation

Close your eyes and bring your attention to your heart centre. Visualise a soft, warm light emanating from your heart, expanding with each breath. As you inhale, imagine this light growing brighter and more vibrant, filling your entire body. As you exhale, release any pain, trauma, or negative emotions, allowing them to dissolve into the light. Repeat this visualisation for a few minutes, feeling your heart becoming lighter and more open.

INSTRUCTIONS

4. Crystal Healing
Hold the rose quartz crystal or any other crystal associated with love and healing in your hands. Close your eyes and connect with its energy. Visualise the crystal radiating a gentle pink light, enveloping your heart in a warm, loving embrace. Feel its healing energy permeating every cell of your body, releasing any energetic blockages and restoring balance. Keep the crystal close to your heart throughout the ritual.

5. Journaling and Release
Take your journal and pen, and write down any emotions, thoughts, or experiences that you wish to release and heal. Allow yourself to express freely, without judgment or limitation. Once you have written everything down, take a moment to read through your words, acknowledging the pain and trauma. Then, with intention, tear the paper into small pieces, symbolising the release of these burdens from your life. Dispose of the torn paper in a way that feels appropriate to you, such as burying it in the Earth or burning it safely.

6. Affirmation and Intention Setting
Hold the rose quartz crystal in your hands once again. Close your eyes and repeat the following affirmation three times:

"I am open to healing. I release the past and embrace love. I am ready to shift my vibration and experience spiritual growth."

INSTRUCTIONS

7. Integration and Gratitude

Take a few moments to sit in silence, allowing the energy of the ritual to integrate within you. Express gratitude for the healing and transformation that has taken place. Thank the elements, crystals, and any spiritual guides or higher powers you connect with for their support and guidance.

Conclusion

As you move forward from this ritual, remember that healing is a continuous journey. Embrace self-care practices, seek support when needed, and nurture yourself with love and compassion. May the Transformational Alchemy of Love guide you towards a healed heart, an elevated vibration, and profound spiritual growth.

CHAPTER 03

03
CHAPTER

Embracing Sacred Connection and Collective Transformation

In the tapestry of our lives, there are moments when we yearn for deeper connections, shared experiences, and the transformative power of collective energy. It is within these sacred spaces of togetherness that we find solace, inspiration, and the opportunity for profound growth. This chapter is a collection of sacred rituals specifically designed for group settings, whether in retreats, sacred circle gatherings, or any gathering of kindred souls.

Each ritual within this chapter is a testament to the power of collective intention, shared energy, and the sacred bonds that form when we come together with open hearts and open minds.

Within these pages, you will discover a variety of rituals that invite you to explore the depths of shared experience, honour the unique gifts each individual brings, and create a container for collective healing and growth. These rituals range from guided meditations and sacred ceremonies to interactive activities and heartfelt discussions, providing a diverse array of tools to support the journey of group exploration.

In the midst of a world that often emphasizes individualism and separation, rituals in group settings become bridges that connect us, reminding us of our shared humanity and the power of unity. They offer us the opportunity to listen deeply, hold space for one another, and witness the beauty and diversity of our collective experiences.

03
CHAPTER

Embracing Sacred Connection and Collective Transformation

As you embark on this journey through the rituals within this chapter, I invite you to approach them with an open heart, a spirit of inclusivity, and a willingness to embrace the transformative power of shared intention. Allow yourself to fully immerse in the collective energy, honouring the wisdom and unique contributions of each participant.

May these sacred rituals serve as gentle guides, fostering deep connections, expanding consciousness, and nurturing the collective transformation that is possible when we come together in sacred space. May they remind us of the profound impact we have on one another and the potential for healing and growth that lies within our shared experiences.

May these rituals be a testament to the power of sacred practices in group settings and a reminder that, when we gather with intention and love, we create a container for profound transformation and collective healing.

With gratitude and blessings.

Sacred Cacao Ceremony
Nurturing Connection & Empowerment in Women's Circle

Introduction

This sacred cacao ceremony is designed to create a safe and nurturing space for women to gather, connect, and empower one another. Cacao, known as the "food of the gods," is used as a heart-opening and grounding tool in this ritual. By engaging in this ceremony, women can deepen their connection with themselves, each other, and the divine feminine energy within.

Materials Needed

1. Cacao: Use high-quality ceremonial-grade cacao, preferably in solid form or as a powdered drink mix.
2. Warm water or plant-based milk: Use this to prepare the cacao beverage.
3. Cups or mugs: Provide each participant with a cup or mug for their cacao.
4. Optional: Sacred objects, crystals, candles, incense, or any other items that evoke a sense of sacredness and support the intention of the ceremony.

INSTRUCTIONS

1. Preparation
   - Set up a sacred space where the women can gather comfortably, either indoors or outdoors.
   - Arrange the sacred objects, crystals, candles, or any other items you have chosen to create a visually appealing and sacred atmosphere.
   - Prepare the cacao beverage according to the instructions provided with the ceremonial-grade cacao.

2. Opening Circle
   - Gather the women in a circle, ensuring that everyone has a clear view and can hear each other.
   - Begin by inviting each woman to briefly introduce herself and share her intention for the ceremony.
   - Encourage an atmosphere of trust, respect, and non-judgment, emphasizing the importance of confidentiality within the circle.

3. Cacao Blessing
   - Hold the container of cacao in your hands and offer a blessing or prayer, inviting the spirit of cacao to support and guide the ceremony.
   - Pass the container around the circle, allowing each woman to hold it and silently offer her own personal intention or prayer.

INSTRUCTIONS

4. Heart Opening Meditation

- Lead the women in a guided meditation focused on opening the heart centre and connecting with their inner wisdom and divine feminine energy.
- Encourage them to visualize a warm, loving light expanding from their hearts and radiating throughout their bodies.

5. Cacao Drinking Ceremony

- Distribute the cups or mugs filled with the prepared cacao beverage to each participant.
- Invite the women to hold their cups close to their hearts, connecting with the energy of the cacao and setting their personal intentions for the ceremony.
- Encourage them to drink the cacao mindfully, savouring each sip and allowing the warmth and nourishment of the cacao to permeate their beings.

6. Sharing and Connection

- After drinking the cacao, invite the women to share their experiences, insights, or any emotions that arose during the meditation and cacao drinking.
- Encourage active listening and support within the circle, allowing each woman to express herself fully and without interruption.
- Remind the participants that sharing is optional, and they can choose to pass if they prefer to keep their experiences private.

INSTRUCTIONS

7. Empowerment Ritual
- Create a ritual that empowers each woman individually or the group as a whole, such as a guided visualisation, affirmation, or symbolic gesture.
- Tailor the ritual to the specific intentions and needs of the women in the circle, allowing them to tap into their inner strength, wisdom, and divine feminine power.

8. Closing Circle
- Conclude the ceremony by gathering the women in a closing circle.
- Offer gratitude for the cacao, the women in the circle, and the divine feminine energy that was invoked and shared.
- Invite each woman to briefly share her reflections on the ceremony and express gratitude for the experience.

Conclusion
By engaging in this sacred cacao ceremony, women can nurture connection, empowerment, and the divine feminine energy within themselves and the circle. Remember to approach this ritual with reverence, authenticity, and an open heart, allowing the cacao to support and guide the experience. Regularly practicing this ceremony can deepen the bond between women, foster personal growth, and create a sacred space for healing, empowerment, and celebration of the divine feminine.

Sacred Pregnancy Circle Ritual
Nurturing the Divine Feminine

Introduction

The Sacred Pregnancy Circle Ritual is a beautiful ceremony designed to honour and celebrate the journey of pregnancy within a group of women. It is a sacred space where expectant mothers can come together, share their experiences, and support one another on their path to motherhood. This ritual can be performed in a serene and comfortable environment, ideally during the later stages of pregnancy.

Materials Needed

1. A clean and quiet space, preferably with cushions or comfortable seating for each participant.
2. Soft lighting, such as candles or fairy lights, to create a warm and inviting atmosphere.
3. A small altar or table adorned with symbols of fertility, motherhood, and the divine feminine.
4. Blankets and pillows for added comfort.
5. A journal or notebook and pens for each participant.
6. Optional: Crystals, flowers, or any other sacred objects that hold personal significance to the participants..

INSTRUCTIONS

Getting Started

The Sacred Pregnancy Circle Ritual is a sacred practice that honours the transformative journey of pregnancy and the power of the divine feminine. It provides a safe and nurturing space for expectant mothers to connect, share, and support one another. May this ritual bring comfort, strength, and a deep sense of community to all who participate.

Preparation

1. Set up the space by arranging the cushions or seating in a circle, ensuring that everyone has enough room to be comfortable.

2. Place the altar or table in the centre of the circle, adorning it with the chosen symbols and objects.

3. Dim the lights and light the candles, creating a soft and soothing ambiance.

4. Arrange the blankets and pillows around the circle, inviting participants to make themselves comfortable.

5. Distribute the journals or notebooks and pens to each participant.

INSTRUCTIONS

The Ritual

1. Begin by gathering in a circle, holding hands if desired, and taking a few deep breaths together to centre and ground yourselves.

2. Invite each participant to share their name, their stage of pregnancy, and any feelings or experiences they would like to express. Encourage active listening and support from the group.

3. As the facilitator, guide the group in a gentle meditation to connect with their own bodies and the life growing within. Encourage participants to visualise a warm and loving light surrounding their womb, nurturing and protecting their baby.

4. Invite each participant to take turns sharing their hopes, dreams, and intentions for their pregnancy and motherhood journey. Encourage them to speak from the heart, expressing their deepest desires and fears without judgment.

5. After each participant shares, the group can offer words of affirmation, support, or blessings. This can be done through gentle touch, a shared mantra, or simply by holding space and sending loving energy.

6. Encourage participants to write down any insights, reflections, or messages they receive during the circle in their journals or notebooks.

INSTRUCTIONS

7. As a group, offer a collective prayer or blessing for the health, well-being, and safe delivery of each participant's baby. This can be done through a shared chant, a guided visualisation, or a simple spoken affirmation.

8. Take a few moments of silence to honour the sacredness of the circle and the divine feminine energy present.

9. Conclude the ritual by expressing gratitude for the shared experience and the support of the group. Encourage participants to continue supporting and uplifting one another throughout their pregnancy journey.

10. Offer a closing prayer or affirmation, expressing gratitude for the divine feminine energy and the gift of life.

11. Gently blow out the candles, symbolizing the completion of the ritual.

12. Allow participants to linger in the space, sharing any final thoughts or experiences if desired.

13. Encourage participants to take their journals or notebooks home with them as a reminder of the sacred circle and the support they have received.

Sacred Pregnancy Circle Ritual
Sacred Meditation Script

Find a comfortable position, either sitting or lying down, and gently close your eyes. Take a deep breath in, filling your lungs with fresh air, and exhale slowly, releasing any tension or stress.

As you continue to breathe deeply, bring your attention to the sacred space within you, where the divine feminine resides. Visualise a soft, warm light glowing in your womb, representing the nurturing energy of creation and the bond with your child.

Imagine yourself surrounded by a circle of women, all connected by the shared experience of pregnancy. Feel the support and love emanating from this circle, knowing that you are not alone on this journey.

Now, bring your attention to the life growing within you. Visualise your child as a radiant light, nestled safely in your womb. Feel the connection between you and your baby, a bond that transcends words and is felt deep within your soul.

As you continue to breathe, imagine a gentle, loving energy flowing from your heart to your womb, enveloping your child in a cocoon of love and protection. Feel the warmth and tenderness of this energy, nurturing both you and your baby.

Take a moment to reflect on the miracle of life and the power of the divine feminine within you. Embrace the strength and wisdom that comes with carrying life, knowing that you are a vessel of creation and love.

Sacred Pregnancy Circle Ritual
Sacred Meditation Script

Now, imagine a golden thread of light connecting you to each woman in the circle. This thread represents the collective strength and support of the sisterhood. Feel the energy of unity and love flowing through this thread, strengthening the bond between you and your fellow mothers-to-be.

Take a few moments to share any thoughts, hopes, or fears that arise within you. Know that this circle is a safe space for you to express yourself and receive support. Feel the power of collective wisdom and love as each woman in the circle holds space for you.

Now, bring your attention back to your breath. Inhale deeply, drawing in love and strength, and exhale, releasing any doubts or worries. Feel the connection between your breath and the life within you, a reminder of the divine dance of creation.

Take a moment to express gratitude for this sacred journey of pregnancy and the opportunity to nurture the divine feminine within you. Know that you are a vessel of love and creation, and your bond with your child is a sacred gift.

When you are ready, gently bring your awareness back to your physical body. Wiggle your fingers and toes, and slowly open your eyes. Carry this sense of connection, love, and strength with you throughout your pregnancy journey, knowing that you are supported by the divine feminine and the sisterhood of mothers.

Blessing Ceremony for a Newborn & Mother

Embracing Love, Protection & Abundance

Introduction

The Blessing Ceremony for a Newborn and Mother is a deeply revered and significant ritual that holds immense importance in many cultures and traditions. This sacred ceremony symbolizes the embrace of love, protection, and abundance for both the child and the mother. It is a joyous celebration of the arrival of a new life, but it also serves as a powerful invocation of blessings for a prosperous and harmonious journey ahead. The ceremony brings together family, friends, and community to offer prayers, blessings, and well-wishes, creating a sacred space filled with love, support, and positive energy for the newborn and the mother as they embark on their new chapter of life.

Select a Suitable Venue

Choose a location that can accommodate the number of participants comfortably. It can be a living room, backyard, community centre, or any space that holds significance for the family. Ensure there is enough seating and space for everyone to gather around the baby and mother.

INSTRUCTIONS

1. Arrange Seating
Set up chairs or cushions in a circle or semi-circle to encourage a sense of unity and connection among the participants. Ensure that the mother and baby have a comfortable and central position within the circle.

2. Create an Altar
Designate a small table or area as an altar where you can place meaningful objects or symbols. This can include a photograph of the baby, a candle, flowers, or any items that hold spiritual or personal significance to the family.

3. Gather Ritual Items
Prepare any ritual items that will be used during the ceremony, such as a candle for lighting, a bowl of water for purification, or any specific items associated with the family's cultural or religious traditions.

4. Create a Program
Develop a program or outline for the ceremony, including the order of rituals, readings, blessings, and any special contributions from participants. Ensure that the program allows for moments of reflection, silence, and personal blessings.

5. Invite Participants
Send out invitations to family members, close friends, and loved ones who would like to be part of this special ceremony. Encourage them to bring their love, positive energy, and blessings to share with the baby and mother.

INSTRUCTIONS

6. Prepare Blessing Cards or Tokens
Provide small cards or tokens to each participant, allowing them to write or express their personal blessings for the baby and mother. These can be collected and presented to the family as a keepsake after the ceremony.

7. Arrange Refreshments
Consider providing light refreshments or a simple meal for participants to enjoy after the ceremony. This allows for further bonding and celebration among the group.

8. Practice Mindfulness and Respect
Remind participants to approach the ceremony with an open heart, mindfulness, and respect for the family's beliefs and traditions. Encourage them to be fully present and engaged in the blessings they offer.

Remember, the most important aspect of setting up a blessing ceremony is to create a loving and sacred space where the baby and mother can be surrounded by the positive energy, love, protection, and abundance of the group.

BLESSING CEREMONY
SACRED SCRIPT

Introduction:
Welcome friends and family, to this sacred gathering as we come together to bless and honour the arrival of a precious new life and the mother who has brought forth this miracle. Today, we unite in love, protection, and abundance, surrounding this child and their mother with our heartfelt blessings. Let us begin this sacred ritual, invoking the divine presence and setting our intentions for this blessed occasion.

Opening Invocation:
(Leader or designated person)
In the presence of the divine, we gather here today,
To bless this newborn child and their mother, we pray.
May love, protection, and abundance forever surround,
As we celebrate this new life, so pure and profound.

Lighting of the Sacred Flame:
(Leader or designated person)
As we light this sacred flame, let it symbolize the eternal light of love, protection, and abundance that will guide and bless this child and their mother throughout their lives. May this flame ignite the hearts of all present, filling them with warmth and divine blessings.

(Begin by lighting a candle or a small flame, allowing it to burn throughout the ceremony.)

INSTRUCTIONS

Blessing of the Newborn:
(Leader or designated person)
Now, let us direct our focus and blessings towards the newborn child. As we gather around, let us extend our hands in a gesture of love and connection, as we send our heartfelt blessings to this precious soul.

(Invite each participant to gently place their hands on or near the baby, offering their blessings silently or aloud.)

Participant 1:
May you be surrounded by love, dear child, throughout your journey. May your heart be filled with compassion, kindness, and empathy, and may you always feel the warmth of love in your life.

Participant 2:
May you be protected, little one, from all harm and negativity. May the divine shield you from any adversity, and may you always find strength and courage to overcome life's challenges.

Participant 3:
May abundance flow into your life, sweet child, in all its forms. May you be blessed with good health, happiness, and prosperity, and may your path be filled with opportunities to grow and thrive.

INSTRUCTIONS

Mother's Blessing:
(Leader or designated person)
Now, let us turn our attention to the mother, who has brought forth this beautiful life into the world. As we gather around her, let us extend our hands in a gesture of support and love, as we send our heartfelt blessings to this courageous woman.

(Invite each participant to gently place their hands on or near the mother, offering their blessings silently or aloud.)

Participant 1:
May you be surrounded by love, dear mother, as you embark on this incredible journey of motherhood. May you find strength, patience, and wisdom in every step, and may your heart overflow with joy and fulfilment.

Participant 2:
May you be protected, nurturing mother, as you care for and guide this precious child. May the divine embrace you with its loving arms, providing you with the support and guidance you need throughout your life.

Participant 3:
May abundance flow into your life, beautiful mother, in all its forms. May you be blessed with good health, prosperity, and fulfilment, and may your life be enriched by the love and joy of your child.

INSTRUCTIONS

Closing Blessing:
(Leader or designated person)
As we conclude this sacred ceremony, let us offer our deepest gratitude to the divine for the gift of life and the love that binds us all. May the blessings bestowed upon this child and their mother today continue to grow and flourish, nurturing their souls and guiding them towards a life filled with love, protection, and abundance.

(Allow a moment of silence for personal reflection and gratitude.)

Closing Prayer:
(Leader or designated person)
With hearts full of love and gratitude, we conclude this sacred ceremony. May the divine presence always be with this child and their mother, guiding them on their journey and showering them with blessings. May their lives be filled with love, protection, and abundance, now and forevermore.

(Blow out the sacred flame, symbolising the completion of the ceremony.)

Note: This ritual can be adapted and personalised according to individual beliefs, cultural practices, and preferences.

Awakening Unity
A Sacred Ritual for Spiritual Retreat

Introduction

This sacred ritual is designed to deepen the spiritual connection and foster unity among participants during a retreat inspired by yogic philosophy. Drawing upon the principles of yoga, including mindfulness, self-reflection, and compassion, this ritual aims to create a sacred space for personal growth, collective harmony, and the exploration of inner wisdom.

Materials Needed

1. Yoga mats or cushions for each participant
2. Soft lighting or candles
3. Incense or essential oils for ambiance
4. A small altar or focal point with symbolic items (e.g., flowers, crystals, statues)
5. Optional: Yoga props (blocks, straps) for individual comfort

INSTRUCTIONS

1. Setting the Sacred Space

- Choose a serene and quiet location for the ritual, preferably in nature or a dedicated meditation space.
- Arrange yoga mats or cushions in a circle, facing inward, creating a sense of unity and connection.
- Place soft lighting or candles around the space, creating a warm and inviting atmosphere.
- If desired, light incense or use essential oils to enhance the ambiance and promote relaxation.

2. Opening Meditation

- Invite participants to find a comfortable seated position on their mats or cushions, with eyes gently closed.
- Guide the group through a grounding meditation, encouraging them to connect with their breath and bring their awareness to the present moment.
- Lead a collective intention-setting, inviting participants to silently reflect on their personal intentions for the retreat and the shared experience.

3. Chanting and Mantra

- Begin the ritual by introducing a simple and meaningful mantra or chant, such as "Om" or "Sat Nam."
- Guide the group in chanting the chosen mantra together, allowing the vibrations to resonate within each participant and throughout the space.
- Encourage participants to focus on the sound and vibration, allowing it to deepen their connection to themselves and the group.

INSTRUCTIONS

4. Yoga Asana Practice
   - Lead a gentle and accessible yoga asana practice, incorporating postures that promote grounding, opening the heart, and cultivating inner strength.
   - Offer modifications and variations to accommodate different levels of experience and physical abilities.
   - Emphasize the importance of mindful movement, breath awareness, and self-compassion throughout the practice.

5. Guided Meditation
   - Transition from the yoga asana practice into a guided meditation, focusing on themes of self-reflection, inner peace, and unity.
   - Guide participants through a visualisation or body scan, encouraging them to explore their inner landscape and connect with their innate wisdom.
   - Offer gentle reminders to let go of judgment, expectations, and distractions, allowing each participant to fully immerse themselves in the present moment.

6. Sharing Circle
   - Create a safe and supportive space for participants to share their experiences, insights, or reflections from the meditation and yoga practice.
   - Encourage active listening and non-judgmental presence as each person shares, fostering a sense of community and mutual support.
   - Remind participants that sharing is optional, and they may choose to simply listen and hold space for others.

INSTRUCTIONS

7. Closing Ceremony
- Gather the group's attention back to the present moment, acknowledging the collective energy and growth experienced during the ritual.
- Invite participants to offer gratitude for the practice, the teachings, and the connections made.
- Conclude the ritual with a final chant or mantra, allowing the vibrations to resonate and seal the intentions set at the beginning.

8. Integration
- Encourage participants to take a few moments of silence and reflection before slowly transitioning back into their daily activities.
- Offer suggestions for integrating the insights and practices from the ritual into their lives during the retreat and beyond.
- Remind participants of the importance of self-care, self-compassion, and continued exploration of yogic philosophy throughout the retreat and beyond.

Note: This ritual is intended to support personal growth and collective unity. It is important to create a safe and inclusive space, respecting individual boundaries and comfort levels. If participants experience any discomfort or distress, provide appropriate support and guidance.

Harmonic Healing
A Sacred Sound Bath

Introduction

This sacred sound bath ritual aims to create a space of deep relaxation, healing, and restoration. Through the power of sound vibrations, it seeks to promote physical, emotional, and spiritual well-being.

Materials Needed

1. Various instruments for sound healing, such as crystal singing bowls, Tibetan singing bowls, chimes, gongs, drums, rattles, or any other instruments that produce soothing sounds.
2. Comfortable mats, cushions, or blankets for participants to lie down or sit on.
3. Optional: Essential oils, incense, or candles to enhance the ambiance.

Preparation
1. Find a quiet and serene space where the sound bath can take place without interruptions.
2. Arrange the instruments in a way that allows easy access and movement around the space.
3. Create a cosy and inviting atmosphere by dimming the lights, lighting candles or incense, and diffusing essential oils if desired.
4. Ensure that participants have comfortable seating or lying arrangements, such as mats, cushions, or blankets.

INSTRUCTIONS

1. Grounding and Intention Setting
  - Begin by inviting participants to find a comfortable position, either lying down or sitting.
  - Guide them through a brief grounding exercise, encouraging them to connect with their breath and the present moment.
  - Invite participants to set their intentions for the sound bath, focusing on their personal healing and well-being.

2. Opening Invocation
  - Offer a short opening prayer, blessing, or intention to create a sacred and safe space for healing.
  - You may choose to call upon any spiritual or divine energies that resonate with you and the participants.

3. Sound Journey
  - Start playing the instruments gently, allowing the sounds to wash over the participants.
  - Begin with soft and soothing tones, gradually building up to more intense or resonant sounds.
  - Explore different rhythms, melodies, and harmonies, allowing the vibrations to penetrate and resonate within the space and the participants' bodies.

INSTRUCTIONS

4. Intuitive Sound Healing
 - Allow yourself to be guided by intuition as you play the instruments.
 - Pay attention to the energy in the room and the responses of the participants.
 - Focus on creating a balance between grounding, calming, and uplifting sounds, adapting to the needs of the group.

5. Individual Attention:
 - If desired, offer individual attention to participants by playing instruments near or over their bodies.
 - Use the instruments to create gentle vibrations and harmonies that can be felt and experienced on a deeper level.
 - Respect personal boundaries and ask for consent before providing individual attention.

6. Silence and Integration:
 - Gradually reduce the intensity of the sounds, allowing the vibrations to fade away.
 - Encourage participants to remain in silence for a few moments, allowing the healing energies to integrate and settle within their bodies and minds.
 - Offer a gentle reminder to honour their experiences and take any necessary time for reflection and self-care.

INSTRUCTIONS

7. Closing and Gratitude

- Offer a closing prayer, blessing, or affirmation, expressing gratitude for the healing energies and experiences shared.
- Invite participants to slowly bring their awareness back to the present moment, gently moving their bodies and stretching if needed.
- Provide a space for participants to share their experiences or insights if they feel comfortable doing so.
- Thank everyone for their presence and participation, acknowledging the collective energy created during the sound bath.

Note: It is essential to create a safe and supportive environment during the sound bath. Respect participants' boundaries and ensure their comfort throughout the experience. Remind participants that healing is a personal journey, and their experiences may vary. Encourage self-care and integration after the sound bath, as it can bring up emotions or release energetic blockages.

Embracing Unity
*A Sacred Commitment Ceremony
with Hand Binding and Nature*

Introduction

This sacred ritual serves as a commitment ceremony, symbolising the union and dedication between two individuals. It incorporates the ancient practice of hand binding, a ritualistic gesture that signifies the joining of two souls. Additionally, the presence of nature enhances the sacredness of the ceremony, connecting the couple to the natural world and its inherent wisdom and blessings.

Materials Needed

1. A serene outdoor location, such as a garden or forest clearing, that resonates with the couple's connection to nature.
2. A small table or altar adorned with flowers, candles, and other natural elements.
3. Two long, soft ribbons or cords, preferably in colours that hold personal significance for the couple.
4. Optional: additional natural elements, such as stones, leaves, or feathers, to enhance the ritual.

INSTRUCTIONS

1. Preparation

a. Choose a location that reflects the couple's connection to nature and provides a sense of tranquillity and sacredness.

b. Set up the small table or altar, arranging flowers, candles, and other natural elements in a way that feels harmonious and meaningful.

2. Opening Invocation

- Gather the couple and any witnesses or loved ones around the altar, forming a close-knit circle.
- Begin with a moment of silence, allowing everyone to ground themselves and connect with the energy of the natural surroundings.
- Offer an invocation or prayer, inviting the presence of divine love and guidance to bless the ceremony.

3. Hand Binding

- Invite the couple to face each other, holding hands.
- Take one of the ribbons or cords and gently wrap it around the couple's hands, starting from the wrists and moving towards the fingertips.
- As you bind their hands together, speak words of commitment, love, and unity. Encourage the couple to express their own vows or promises to each other.
- Tie a secure knot at the fingertips, symbolising the strength and permanence of their bond.

INSTRUCTIONS

4. Nature's Blessings
 - Invite the couple to step away from the altar and into nature, holding hands and still bound by the ribbon or cord.
 - Encourage them to walk together, exploring the natural surroundings and connecting with the elements.
 - As they walk, invite the couple to share their hopes, dreams, and intentions for their shared journey, speaking them aloud or silently in their hearts.
 - Encourage them to find a natural element that resonates with their intentions, such as a stone, leaf, or feather, and hold it close to their hearts.

5. Unity Ritual
 - Return to the altar, still holding hands and bound by the ribbon or cord.
 - Invite the couple to place their chosen natural elements on the altar, symbolising the merging of their intentions and the blessings of nature.
 - Encourage them to speak words of gratitude and appreciation for the natural world and its role in their commitment.
 - Untie the ribbon or cord, releasing their hands while keeping the knot intact, signifying their continued connection and commitment.

INSTRUCTIONS

6. Closing and Celebration
   a. Gather the circle once again around the altar, holding hands or placing hands on each other's shoulders.
   b. Offer a closing prayer or blessing, expressing gratitude for the union of the couple and the blessings of nature.
   c. Celebrate the commitment with joyful music, dance, or a shared meal, honouring the love and unity that has been celebrated.

Remember, this ritual is a guide, and it can be adapted to suit the couple's beliefs and preferences. The intention is to create a sacred space that honours the commitment between two individuals, incorporating the ancient practice of hand binding and the blessings of nature. May this ceremony strengthen their bond and deepen their connection to each other and the natural world.

Embracing Unity
A Sacred Script
with Hand Binding and Nature

Introduction

This sacred ritual script is designed to be used during a hand binding ceremony in nature, symbolising the union and commitment between two individuals. The ceremony takes place in a serene outdoor location, allowing the couple to connect with the natural world and its inherent wisdom and blessings.

Preparation

- Choose a serene outdoor location that resonates with the couple's connection to nature.
- Set up a small altar adorned with flowers, candles, and other natural elements.
- Place two long, soft ribbons or cords on the altar, preferably in colours that hold personal significance for the couple.

INSTRUCTIONS

Opening Invocation

Officiant: (Standing at the altar) Welcome, beloved friends and witnesses, to this sacred hand binding ceremony in nature. We gather here today to witness and celebrate the union of [Partner 1's name] and [Partner 2's name]. Let us take a moment to ground ourselves and connect with the energy of the natural surroundings.

(Pause for a moment of silence)

Officiant: We invite the presence of divine love and guidance to bless this ceremony and the commitment being made. Let us begin.

Hand Binding

Officiant: [Partner 1's name] and [Partner 2's name], please face each other and hold hands.

(The couple faces each other, holding hands)

Officiant: (Taking one of the ribbons or cords) This ribbon represents the joining of your lives, the intertwining of your souls. As I bind your hands together, I invite you to express your vows or promises to each other.

(Officiant gently wraps the ribbon or cord around the couple's hands, starting from the wrists and moving towards the fingertips)

INSTRUCTIONS

Officiant: [Partner 1's name], please repeat after me: I, [Partner 1's name], take you, [Partner 2's name], to be my beloved partner.

Partner 1: I, [Partner 1's name], take you, [Partner 2's name], to be my beloved partner.

Officiant: [Partner 2's name], please repeat after me: I, [Partner 2's name], take you, [Partner 1's name], to be my beloved partner.

Partner 2: I, [Partner 2's name], take you, [Partner 1's name], to be my beloved partner.

Officiant: (Tying a secure knot at the fingertips) With this knot, your hands are bound together, symbolizing the strength and permanence of your bond. May your love and commitment grow deeper with each passing day.

Nature's Blessings
Officiant: Now, I invite you to step away from the altar and into nature, still holding hands and bound by the ribbon or cord. As you walk together, feel the presence of the natural world surrounding you, supporting you, and blessing your union.
(The couple walks together, exploring the natural surroundings)

Officiant: [Partner 1's name] and [Partner 2's name], as you walk in nature, share your hopes, dreams, and intentions for your shared journey. Speak them aloud or silently in your hearts.

(The couple shares their intentions and aspirations)

INSTRUCTIONS

Officiant: Now, find a natural element that resonates with your intentions, such as a stone, leaf, or feather. Hold it close to your hearts, feeling the energy and blessings it carries.

(The couple finds their chosen natural elements and holds them close to their hearts)

Unity Ritual
Officiant: Return to the altar, still holding hands and bound by the ribbon or cord. Place your chosen natural elements on the altar, symbolising the merging of your intentions and the blessings of nature.

(The couple places their chosen natural elements on the altar)

Officiant: (Untying the ribbon or cord, releasing their hands while keeping the knot intact) With this act, your hands are released, but the knot remains, signifying your continued connection and commitment. May your love and unity be forever strong.

Closing and Celebration
Officiant: Beloved friends and witnesses, we have witnessed the sacred hand binding ceremony in nature, celebrating the union of [Partner 1's name] and [Partner 2's name]. Let us offer a closing prayer or blessing, expressing gratitude for their commitment and the blessings of nature.

INSTRUCTIONS

(Officiant offers a closing prayer or blessing)

Officiant: Now, let us celebrate this joyous occasion with music, dance, or a shared meal, honouring the love and unity that has been celebrated.

(As the ceremony concludes, the couple and guests celebrate and rejoice)

May this sacred hand binding ceremony in nature strengthen the bond between [Partner 1's name] and [Partner 2's name], and may their love and commitment continue to grow and flourish in harmony with the natural world.

Sacred Ritual for a Men's Circle
Honouring Masculinity & Facilitating Healing

In a world where the concept of masculinity is often misunderstood or misrepresented, there is a growing need for spaces that honour and celebrate the essence of manhood. The sacred ritual of a men's circle provides a powerful platform for men to come together, connect, and heal.

This ancient practice acknowledges the unique challenges and experiences faced by men, offering a safe and supportive environment for them to explore their emotions, vulnerabilities, and strengths.

Through guided discussions, storytelling, and various healing modalities, this sacred ritual aims to foster a deeper understanding of masculinity, promote personal growth, and cultivate a sense of brotherhood.

 It is a transformative journey that empowers men to embrace their authentic selves and navigate the complexities of life with grace and integrity.

.

Sacred Ritual for a Men's Circle
SETUP GUIDELINES

1. Space: Choose a quiet and comfortable indoor location where participants can feel safe and at ease. Ensure there is enough space for everyone to sit comfortably in a circle.

2. Seating: Arrange chairs in a circle to promote equality and encourage open communication. Make sure there are enough chairs for all participants.

3. Altar: Create a central altar as a focal point for the circle. Decorate it with meaningful objects such as candles, crystals, symbols of masculinity, and natural elements like stones or plants.

4. Sacred Objects: Include items that hold significance for the participants, such as feathers, drums, or ritual tools. These can be used during the ceremony or as personal offerings.

5. Ritual Tools: Provide tools like sage or palo santo for smudging, a ceremonial bowl for offerings, and a bell or chime to mark the beginning and end of the circle.

6. Writing Materials: Have pens, paper, and journals available for participants to reflect on their experiences or write down any insights during the circle.

7. Lighting: Create a warm and inviting ambiance with soft lighting, such as candles or dimmed overhead lights.

Sacred Ritual for a Men's Circle
SETUP GUIDELINES

8. Music: Prepare a playlist of soothing and instrumental music to create a calming atmosphere during the circle.

9. Refreshments: Offer light refreshments like water, herbal tea, or healthy snacks to nourish participants during breaks.

10. Guidelines: Prepare a set of guidelines or agreements that promote respect, active listening, confidentiality, and non-judgment within the circle. Display them visibly for everyone to see.

By following these instructions, you can create a safe and sacred space for men to honour their masculinity, connect with one another, and facilitate healing.

INSTRUCTIONS

Introduction:
Welcome, brothers, to this sacred gathering of men. Today, we come together to honour our masculinity, to embrace our vulnerabilities, and to support one another on our healing journeys. In this safe and sacred space, we will engage in a ritual that allows us to connect deeply with ourselves and each other, fostering healing and growth. Let us begin this sacred ritual, invoking the divine presence and setting our intentions for this transformative experience.

Opening Invocation:
(Leader or designated person)
In the presence of the divine masculine, we gather here today,
To honour our masculinity and heal in a sacred way.
May our hearts open wide, our spirits be free,
As we embark on this journey of healing and unity.

Creating a Sacred Circle:
(Leader or designated person)
Let us form a circle, symbolising the unity and equality among us. As we join hands or place our hands on each other's shoulders, let us feel the strength and support of our brothers. Together, we create a safe and sacred container for healing and transformation.

(Invite participants to form a circle, either by joining hands or placing hands on each other's shoulders.)

INSTRUCTIONS

Sharing Our Intentions:
(Leader or designated person)
Now, let us take a moment to reflect on our intentions for this ritual. What do you seek to heal or release? What aspects of your masculinity do you wish to honour and embrace? In a moment of silence, connect with your heart and set your intention for this sacred gathering.

(Allow a few moments of silence for participants to reflect on their intentions.)

Sharing Circle:
(Leader or designated person)
In this sharing circle, we invite each brother to speak from the heart, sharing their intentions, experiences, or any challenges they wish to heal. This is a space of non-judgment, compassion, and deep listening. Each brother will have the opportunity to speak while others hold space and offer their support.

(Start the sharing circle, allowing each participant to speak one at a time. Encourage active listening and remind participants to hold space for each other without interrupting or offering advice.)

Ritual of Release:
(Leader or designated person)
Now, let us release any burdens, wounds, or limiting beliefs that no longer serve us. Each brother will have the opportunity to step into the centre of the circle and share what they wish to release. As they speak, let us hold them in our hearts and offer our support.

INSTRUCTIONS

(Invite each participant, one at a time, to step into the center of the circle and share what they wish to release. Encourage them to speak from their hearts and allow emotions to flow freely.)

Group Healing Meditation:
(Leader or designated person)
In this guided meditation, we will collectively channel healing energy towards each brother, supporting their journey of healing and growth. Close your eyes, take deep breaths, and allow yourself to be fully present in this moment.

(Lead a guided meditation, focusing on sending healing energy, love, and support to each participant. Encourage participants to visualize the healing energy enveloping them and releasing any pain or wounds.)

Closing Blessing:
(Leader or designated person)
As we conclude this sacred ritual, let us offer our deepest gratitude to the divine masculine for guiding and supporting us on our healing journeys. May we continue to honour and embrace our masculinity, nurturing ourselves and each other with love, compassion, and understanding.

(Allow a moment of silence for personal reflection and gratitude.)

INSTRUCTIONS

Closing Prayer:
(Leader or designated person)
With hearts full of gratitude and brotherhood, we conclude this sacred ritual. May the divine masculine continue to guide us, heal us, and unite us as brothers. May we carry the lessons and blessings of this gathering into our lives, spreading healing and love wherever we go.

(Release the circle by letting go of each other's hands or shoulders.)

Note: This ritual can be adapted and personalised according to the specific needs, beliefs, and preferences of the men's circle. It is important to create a safe and supportive environment where participants feel comfortable sharing and healing.

Sacred Ritual for a Men's Circle
Sacred Meditation Script

Welcome to this sacred men's circle, a space dedicated to honouring masculinity and cultivating healing. Find a comfortable position, allowing your body to relax and your breath to deepen. Close your eyes and bring your attention to the present moment.

Take a deep breath in, feeling the air fill your lungs, and exhale, releasing any tension or stress. With each breath, let go of any expectations or judgments, allowing yourself to fully immerse in this healing meditation.

Visualise a warm, golden light surrounding you, enveloping you in a cocoon of love and acceptance. Feel this light radiating from your heart, connecting you to the divine masculine energy within.

As you breathe, imagine this golden light expanding, reaching out to all the men in this circle, creating a powerful bond of brotherhood and support. Feel the strength and unity that comes from honouring and embracing masculinity in its true essence.

Now, bring your attention to any areas of your life where healing is needed. It could be emotional wounds, past traumas, or limiting beliefs that no longer serve you. Allow these experiences to come to the surface, acknowledging them with compassion and understanding.

Sacred Ritual for a Men's Circle
Sacred Meditation Script

With each breath, imagine this golden light penetrating these areas of healing, gently soothing and transforming them. Feel the energy of healing and renewal flowing through your body, releasing any pain or burdens you may carry.

As you continue to breathe, affirm to yourself: "I am worthy of healing. I embrace my masculinity with love and compassion. I release any limitations and step into my true power."

Take a moment to reflect on the strength and resilience that resides within you. Recognise the unique gifts and qualities that make you a powerful force in the world. Embrace your role as a protector, provider, and nurturer, knowing that your presence is valuable and needed.

Now, imagine this golden light expanding beyond this circle, radiating out into the world, touching the lives of others with love and healing. Visualise a ripple effect, as the healing energy spreads far and wide, creating a positive impact on the collective consciousness.

Take a few more deep breaths, feeling the energy of healing and transformation integrating into every cell of your being. When you are ready, gently open your eyes, carrying this sense of healing and honour for masculinity with you throughout your day.

Sacred Ritual for a Men's Circle
Sacred Meditation Script

Remember, you are a vital part of this sacred men's circle, and your healing journey contributes to the healing of all. Embrace your masculinity, cultivate healing, and continue to honour the divine essence within you.

CHAPTER

04

CHAPTER

Awakening the Heart
Five-Minute Morning Sacred Rituals

The morning holds a special place in our lives. It is a time of new beginnings, fresh possibilities, and the dawning of a brand-new day. Yet, all too often, we rush through our mornings, barely taking a moment to acknowledge the sacredness of this precious time.

What if we could reclaim our mornings as sacred space, dedicating just a few minutes to nourishing our souls, harmonizing our energy, and inviting the sacred back into our everyday lives?

What if we could infuse our mornings with intention, creation, mindfulness, and heart connection in just five minutes?

By practicing a sacred ritual everyday, you are inviting loving alignment into your life and making sacred time to listen to the whispers of your soul.

Let us bring back the sacred, honour our hearts, and live with love.

Embracing the Sacred Sunrise
A 5-Minute Morning Ritual

Introduction:

Welcome to this sacred morning ritual, designed to honour the beauty and power of the sunrise. In just five minutes, we will connect with the energy of the rising sun, setting our intentions for the day ahead and cultivating a sense of gratitude and peace. Find a quiet space where you can comfortably sit or stand, and let us begin.

Step 1: Centering Breath (1 minute)
Close your eyes and take a deep breath in, feeling the air fill your lungs. Exhale slowly, releasing any tension or worries. Repeat this deep breath three times, allowing your body and mind to relax. As you breathe, imagine yourself becoming more present and attuned to the energy of the morning.

Step 2: Greeting the Sun (1 minute)
Open your eyes and face the direction where the sun is rising. Extend your arms outwards, palms facing up, as if you are embracing the sun's rays. Visualise the warm, golden light enveloping your entire being. In your mind, silently greet the sun with gratitude and reverence for its life-giving energy.

EMBRACING THE SACRED SUNRISE A 5-MINUTE MORNING RITUAL

Step 3: Setting Intentions (2 minutes)
With your arms still extended, take a moment to reflect on what you wish to manifest and experience throughout the day. What qualities do you want to embody? What goals or aspirations do you have? Speak your intentions aloud or silently, infusing them with conviction and positivity. For example, you might say, "I intend to approach today with love, compassion, and a sense of purpose."

Step 4: Gratitude Meditation (1 minute)
Bring your hands to your heart centre, palms pressed together. Close your eyes and take a moment to express gratitude for the blessings in your life. Reflect on the beauty of the sunrise, the gift of a new day, and the opportunities that lie ahead. Allow a sense of gratitude to fill your heart, radiating throughout your entire being.

Conclusion:
As this sacred morning ritual comes to a close, take a final deep breath in, and exhale slowly, releasing any remaining tension or stress. Carry the energy of the sunrise with you throughout the day, allowing it to guide and inspire you. Remember, each morning is a chance for renewal and growth. Embrace the sacredness of the sunrise, and let it illuminate your path.

Harmonising the Day
A 5-Minute Morning Ritual with Crystal Singing Bowl

Introduction

Welcome to this sacred morning ritual, designed to create harmonic energy for your day using the soothing vibrations of a crystal singing bowl. In just five minutes, we will connect with the healing power of sound, setting the tone for a balanced and peaceful day ahead. Find a quiet space where you can comfortably sit, and let us begin.

Step 1: Grounding and Centering (1 minute)
Sit comfortably with your back straight and feet firmly planted on the ground. Take a few deep breaths, allowing your body to relax and your mind to settle. Close your eyes and visualise roots growing from the soles of your feet, grounding you deep into the earth. Feel the stability and support of the earth beneath you.

Step 2: Crystal Singing Bowl Activation (2 minutes)
Hold your crystal singing bowl in your hands, gently tapping it with the mallet to activate its sound. Allow the vibrations to resonate through your body, starting from your hands and spreading throughout your entire being. Close your eyes and focus on the sound, letting it wash over you, bringing a sense of calm and harmony.

HARMONIZING THE DAY: A 5-MINUTE MORNING RITUAL WITH CRYSTAL SINGING BOWL

Step 3: Intention Setting (1 minute)
With the singing bowl still resonating, take a moment to set your intentions for the day. Reflect on what you wish to cultivate and experience. What qualities do you want to embody? What energy do you want to attract? Silently or aloud, state your intentions, infusing them with positivity and clarity. For example, you might say, "I intend to approach this day with grace, love, and openness."

Step 4: Harmonising Meditation (1 minute)
As the singing bowl continues to vibrate, focus your attention on your breath. Inhale deeply, and as you exhale, imagine the sound of the singing bowl harmonising and balancing your energy. Visualise any tension or discord within you being transformed into a state of harmony and peace. Allow the sound to guide you into a meditative state, where you can experience a deep sense of tranquillity.

Conclusion
As this sacred morning ritual comes to a close, gently bring your attention back to the present moment. Take a final deep breath in, and exhale slowly, releasing any remaining tension or stress. Feel the harmonising energy of the crystal singing bowl resonating within you, carrying its healing vibrations throughout your day. Carry this sense of balance and peace with you, knowing that you have set the foundation for a harmonious and fulfilling day ahead.

Heart-Centred Abundance
*A 5-Minute Morning Ritual
to Invite Flow and Prosperity*

Introduction
Welcome to this sacred morning ritual, designed to open your heart and invite abundance to flow into your life. In just five minutes, we will connect with the power of the heart centre, cultivating a sense of gratitude and abundance. Find a quiet space where you can comfortably sit or stand, and let us begin.

Step 1: Centering Breath (1 minute)
Close your eyes and take a deep breath in, feeling the air fill your lungs. Exhale slowly, releasing any tension or worries. Repeat this deep breath three times, allowing your body and mind to relax. As you breathe, imagine your heart centre expanding and opening, ready to receive the abundance that awaits you.

Step 2: Gratitude Practice (2 minutes)
Place your hands over your heart, feeling the warmth and energy radiating from this sacred space. Take a moment to express gratitude for the blessings in your life. Reflect on the abundance that already exists, both big and small. Silently or aloud, express gratitude for the love, opportunities, and resources that flow to you. Allow the feeling of gratitude to fill your heart, amplifying its energy.

HEART-CENTERED ABUNDANCE: A 5-MINUTE MORNING RITUAL TO INVITE FLOW AND PROSPERITY

Step 3: Heart Visualisation (1 minute)
With your hands still over your heart, visualise a bright, golden light emanating from your heart centre. See this light expanding and radiating outward, creating a magnetic field of love and abundance. Visualise this light attracting opportunities, resources, and experiences that align with your highest good. Feel the energy of abundance flowing towards you, knowing that you are deserving and open to receive.

Step 4: Affirmation and Intention (1 minute)
Repeat a positive affirmation that aligns with your desire for abundance. For example, you might say, "I am open to receiving abundance in all areas of my life. I attract opportunities and resources that support my highest good. I am worthy of abundance and prosperity." Set the intention to carry this energy of abundance with you throughout the day, attracting positive experiences and opportunities.

Conclusion
As this sacred morning ritual comes to a close, take a final deep breath in, and exhale slowly, feeling the energy of abundance and gratitude flowing through your entire being. Carry this heart-centred energy with you throughout the day, knowing that you are aligned with the flow of abundance. Trust in the universe's support and guidance, and remain open to the opportunities and blessings that come your way. Embrace the abundance that is already present and the abundance that is yet to come.

Shielding and Protecting
*A 5-Minute Morning Ritual
to Protect Your Energy*

Introduction
Welcome to this sacred morning ritual, designed to help you shield and protect your energy for the day ahead. In just five minutes, we will create a sacred space and establish energetic boundaries to safeguard your well-being. Find a quiet space where you can comfortably sit or stand, and let us begin.

Step 1: Grounding and Centering (1 minute)
Close your eyes and take a deep breath in, feeling the air fill your lungs. Exhale slowly, releasing any tension or distractions. Visualize roots growing from the soles of your feet, extending deep into the earth, anchoring you to its stable and grounding energy. Feel yourself becoming centred and connected.

Step 2: Sacred Space Creation (1 minute)
Envision a sphere of protective light surrounding you, extending from the ground beneath your feet to above your head. See this sphere as a shield of divine energy, impenetrable to any negativity or unwanted influences. Allow this sphere to expand and fill the space around you, creating a sacred and protected space.

SHIELDING AND PROTECTING: A 5-MINUTE MORNING RITUAL TO PROTECT YOUR ENERGY

Step 3: Energetic Cleansing (1 minute)
Imagine a beam of pure, white light descending from above, passing through your body from the crown of your head to the soles of your feet. As this light moves through you, visualize it cleansing and purifying your energy field, removing any stagnant or negative energy. Feel yourself becoming lighter and more vibrant with each breath.

Step 4: Setting Energetic Boundaries (1 minute)
With your eyes still closed, visualize a golden light emanating from your heart centre, expanding outward to form a protective boundary around you. See this boundary as a shield that allows positive energy to flow in while repelling any negativity or unwanted influences. Set the intention that only love, light, and positivity may enter your energetic space.

Step 5: Affirmation and Gratitude (1 minute)
Repeat a positive affirmation to reinforce your energetic protection. For example, you might say, "I am surrounded by divine light and love. My energy is shielded and protected, allowing only positive and uplifting experiences to come my way." Express gratitude for the opportunity to protect your energy and for the blessings that await you throughout the day.

SHIELDING AND PROTECTING: A 5-MINUTE MORNING RITUAL TO PROTECT YOUR ENERGY

Conclusion

As this sacred morning ritual comes to a close, take a final deep breath in, and exhale slowly, feeling the strength and protection of your energetic shield. Carry this sense of empowerment and boundary-setting with you throughout the day, knowing that you have taken the necessary steps to protect your energy and well-being. Trust in the divine guidance and support that surrounds you, and embrace the positive experiences that come your way.

A Five-Minute Morning Sacred Ritual for Heart Protection

Introduction
Welcome to this five-minute morning sacred ritual designed to promote heart protection and overall well-being. By incorporating these simple practices into your daily routine, you can cultivate a sense of inner peace, gratitude, and mindfulness. Let us begin.

Step 1: Setting the Space (1 minute)
Find a quiet and comfortable space where you can sit or stand without distractions. Light a candle or incense, creating an atmosphere of tranquillity. Take a deep breath, allowing yourself to let go of any tension or worries from the previous day.

Step 2: Gratitude Meditation (2 minutes)
Close your eyes and take a few deep breaths, grounding yourself in the present moment. Bring to mind three things you are grateful for today. It could be something as simple as the warmth of the sun, the love of a family member, or the gift of a new day. As you reflect on these blessings, feel your heart fill with gratitude and appreciation.

A FIVE-MINUTE MORNING SACRED RITUAL FOR HEART PROTECTION

Step 3: Heart-Opening Yoga Pose (1 minute)
Stand tall with your feet hip-width apart. Inhale deeply, lifting your arms overhead, palms facing each other. As you exhale, gently arch your back, opening your chest and heart towards the sky. Allow your head to fall back slightly, if comfortable. Hold this pose for a few breaths, feeling a gentle stretch in your chest and heart space. With each breath, imagine your heart expanding with love and compassion.

Step 4: Affirmations for Heart Health (1 minute)
Sit comfortably and place your hands over your heart. Repeat the following affirmations silently or aloud, allowing their positive energy to resonate within you:

- "My heart is strong and healthy."
- "I am open to giving and receiving love."
- "I choose to live with a grateful heart."
- "I am worthy of love and happiness."
- "I release any tension or stress from my heart."

Step 5: Closing and Intention Setting (30 seconds)
Take a final deep breath, feeling the energy of your heart centre. Set an intention for the day, such as "I will prioritise self-care and make heart-healthy choices." Gently open your eyes, bringing this intention with you as you begin your day.

A FIVE-MINUTE MORNING SACRED RITUAL FOR HEART PROTECTION

Conclusion

Congratulations on completing this five-minute morning sacred ritual for heart protection. By incorporating these practices into your daily routine, you are nurturing your heart's well-being and cultivating a sense of inner peace. Remember, the key to heart protection lies in gratitude, mindfulness, and self-care. May your heart be filled with love, joy, and vitality throughout the day.

A Five-Minute Morning Heart-Based Sacred Ritual for Anxiety Relief

Introduction
Welcome to this five-minute morning sacred ritual designed to promote heart-based healing and ease anxiety. By incorporating these simple practices into your daily routine, you can cultivate a sense of calm, balance, and emotional well-being. Let us begin.

Step 1: Setting the Space (1 minute)
Find a quiet and comfortable space where you can sit or stand without distractions. Light a candle or incense, creating an atmosphere of tranquillity. Take a deep breath, allowing yourself to let go of any tension or worries from the previous day.

Step 2: Heart-Centred Breathing (1 minute)
Close your eyes and place your hands over your heart. Take a slow, deep breath in through your nose, allowing your chest and heart to expand. Hold the breath for a moment, and then exhale slowly through your mouth, releasing any tension or anxiety. Repeat this heart-centred breathing for a few cycles, focusing on the soothing rhythm of your breath.

A FIVE-MINUTE MORNING HEART-BASED SACRED RITUAL FOR ANXIETY RELIEF

Step 3: Tapping for Anxiety Relief (2 minutes)
Gently tap on your chest, over your heart, using your fingertips or a soft fist. As you tap, repeat a calming affirmation or mantra, such as "I am safe and at peace" or "I release anxiety and embrace serenity." Feel the vibrations of the tapping resonating through your chest, soothing and grounding your energy. Continue tapping and repeating the affirmation for a couple of minutes, allowing the anxiety to melt away.

Step 4: Gratitude Meditation (1 minute)
With your hands still over your heart, bring to mind three things you are grateful for today. It could be the support of loved ones, the beauty of nature, or the simple pleasures in your life. As you focus on these blessings, feel your heart fill with gratitude and warmth. Allow this gratitude to replace any lingering anxiety or worry.

Step 5: Closing and Intention Setting (30 seconds)
Take a final deep breath, feeling the energy of your heart centre. Set an intention for the day, such as "I choose to approach challenges with a calm and open heart" or "I prioritise self-care and emotional well-being." Gently open your eyes, carrying this intention with you as you begin your day.

A FIVE-MINUTE MORNING HEART-BASED SACRED RITUAL FOR ANXIETY RELIEF

Conclusion

Congratulations on completing this five-minute morning heart-based sacred ritual for anxiety relief. By incorporating these practices into your daily routine, you are nurturing your heart's well-being and cultivating a sense of calm and balance.

Remember, the key to easing anxiety lies in heart-centred breathing, tapping, gratitude, and setting positive intentions. May your heart be filled with peace, love, and serenity throughout the day.

1-Minute Ritual to Bless Your Drinking Water
Pure Health and Harmonic Energy

Introduction

Welcome to the transformative practice of a 1-minute sacred ritual to bless your drinking water for pure health and harmonic energy. In this brief and impactful ritual, we will combine intention, ancient wisdom, and even scientific understanding to enhance the energetic properties of the water you consume. By infusing your water with positive vibrations, you can align it with your well-being and overall harmony.

Science has shown that water is an amazing and powerful substance, capable of holding and transmitting energy. Just as water can be affected by external factors, such as pollutants or negative thoughts, it can also be influenced by positive intentions and uplifting energies. By consciously blessing our drinking water, we can utilise this knowledge and enhance its molecular structure.

Through this ritual, you will have the opportunity to experience the profound effects of intentional blessings on water. By aligning the molecular structure of the water with pure health and harmonic energy, you can tap into its transformative potential and make it an ally in your well-being journey.

1-MINUTE RITUAL TO BLESS YOUR DRINKING WATER PURE HEALTH AND HARMONIC ENERGY

As you engage in this 1-minute sacred ritual, remember that your intentions matter. Embrace the power of your thoughts and emotions, and believe in the positive impact they can have on the water you consume. By embracing intentionality and holistic practices, you become an active participant in your health and well-being.

Now, let us begin this sacred ritual and unlock the potential of your drinking water for pure health and harmonic energy.

Ritual

1. Find a quiet and peaceful space where you can focus on the ritual without distractions.

2. Take a few deep breaths to centre yourself and calm your mind.

3. Hold the glass or bottle of water in both hands and close your eyes.

4. Visualise a bright, radiant light surrounding the water, purifying it and removing any impurities or negative energies.

5. Now, imagine that light entering the water and infusing it with pure, vibrant health and harmonic energy.

1-MINUTE RITUAL TO BLESS YOUR DRINKING WATER PURE HEALTH AND HARMONIC ENERGY

6. As you hold the water, say a simple blessing or affirmation, such as "I bless this water with love and light. May it nourish and revitalise my body, bringing me pure health and harmonic energy."

7. Feel a sense of gratitude and appreciation for the water and its transformative properties.

8. Take a moment to connect with your intentions for drinking the water and the positive effects it will have on your well-being.

9. When you're ready, open your eyes, and drink the blessed water slowly and mindfully, savouring each sip.

10. Express gratitude once again for the water and the nourishment it provides.

Remember, this ritual is intended to be a practice of intention and mindfulness. Embrace the belief that your intentions have the power to influence and enhance the water's properties for your well-being.

"Who can say where
the path will go?

Philosophers guess
but they just don't know."

Hayd

www.embracingsacredrituals.com

www.ingramcontent.com/pod-product-compliance
Lightning Source LLC
Chambersburg PA
CBHW041615220426
43670CB00004B/55